Riding Yorkshire's Final Steam Trains

Riding Yorkshire's Final Steam Trains

Journeys on BR's North Eastern Region

Keith Widdowson

This book is dedicated to my ever-understanding wife Joan. Prior to meeting me the steam locomotive was an unknown subject to her. Now, after trailing around the country over the years with her 'chaser' husband, her own red-lined catches must surely rival that of any other woman's! She also had a hand in selecting the photographs for this book when decisions involving duplication were involved.

Cover illustrations
Front: Normanton-allocated LMS Ivatt 2-6-0 43043 rests at York on 22 April 1967 having arrived with the 04 25 from Manchester Victoria. (Author's collection) *Back*: The geographic area covered within this book is depicted on this 1959 map of the North Eastern Region system map – as extracted from the rear of the public timetable. (Author's collection)

First published 2015
Reprinted, 2019

The History Press
97 St George's Street, Cheltenham,
Gloucestershire, GL50 3QB
www.thehistorypress.co.uk

© Keith Widdowson, 2015

The right of Keith Widdowson to be identified as the Author of this work has been asserted in accordance with the Copyright, Designs and Patents Act 1988.

All rights reserved. No part of this book may be reprinted or reproduced or utilised in any form or by any electronic, mechanical or other means, now known or hereafter invented, including photocopying and recording, or in any information storage or retrieval system, without the permission in writing from the Publishers.

British Library Cataloguing in Publication Data.
A catalogue record for this book is available from the British Library.

ISBN 978 0 7509 6047 2

Typesetting and origination by The History Press
Printed in Great Britain by TJ International Ltd. Padstow, Cornwall.

Contents

	About the Author	7
	Introduction	9
1	Chasing: An Addiction Explained	13
2	A Southerner Ventures 'Abroad'	20
3	Planning the Attack	27
4	Here We Go	31
5	The Last Remaining Outposts	36
6	The Main Players	39
7	Disappointments Galore	44
8	The Alnwick Adventure	64
9	Where Are Those Elusive Jubilees?	70
10	Riding Yorkshire's Nocturnal Mail Trains	90
11	All Aboard the Rail Tours	100
12	Brief Encounters	116
13	No More Wakefield Portions	121
14	The West Riding Finale	134
15	And Still They Come	141
	An Afterthought	147
	Glossary	153
	Appendices	157
	Sources	173

About the Author

Keith Widdowson was born, to his pharmacist father and secretarial mother, during the calamitous winter of 1947 at St Mary Cray, Kent – attending the nearby schools of Poverest and Charterhouse. He joined British Railways in June 1962 as an enquiry clerk at the Waterloo telephone bureau – 'because his mother had noted his obsession with collecting timetables'.

Thus began a forty-five-year career within various train planning departments throughout BR, the bulk of which was at Waterloo but also included locations at Cannon Street, Wimbledon, Crewe, Euston, Blackfriars, Paddington and finally Croydon – specialising in dealing with train crew arrangements. After spending several years during the '70s and '80s in Cheshire, London and Sittingbourne, he returned to his roots in 1985 where he finally met the steading influence in his life, Joan, with whom he had a daughter, Victoria. In addition to membership of the local residents' association (St Paul's Cray), the Sittingbourne & Kemsley Light Railway and the U3A organisation, he keeps busy writing articles for railway magazines and gardening.

INTRODUCTION

FIRSTLY DEAR READER I have a confession to make: I am a baby boomer! Upon returning from active service in the Second World War my dad, who had met my mum just prior to the commencement of hostilities, was one of the fortunate to return safely and set about making a fresh start in the country for which he had fought for freedom. Then I came along in 1947. Why am I relating this seemingly irrelevant information to you in a book about steam travels you may ask? Fast-forward to the mid 1960s and now being a teenager with disposable income and no financial responsibilities, i.e. wives/children/mortgages, the world was my oyster.

I had joined British Railways in 1962 and, although the clerical grading pay structure wasn't the highest paid profession, if the related free and privilege ticket perks associated with the job were utilised to their fullest extent then the ability to travel and see not only Britain but Europe as well would have been foolish to ignore. We were a fortunate generation.

The swinging '60s were a time of full employment and us teenagers had a pocketful of money to spend on whatever we wanted. Released from parental imposition of short back and sides, and obviously influenced by the pop groups of the day, collar length hair and sideboards were grown. Sure I could have spent my wages on girls or cars or other recreational pursuits – but they could, and indeed did, wait. As a 17-year-old in 1964 the world was there for a teenager full of wanderlust and youthful vigour to explore. There was, however, a more significant matter that necessitated my attention. The steam locomotive was fast disappearing and locating and travelling with them took priority over everything else. Had teenage 'freedom' and the death throes of the Iron Horse[*] not coincided during this period then it would be unlikely that books such as this would have been penned.

---

[*] An 'Iron Horse' is an iconic literary term widely popularised and found frequently in use during the one and half centuries following the competition win by George Stephenson's Rocket. In the 1860s railroads were built across North America – the Native Americans hating this intrusion. Because initially the train cars were pulled along the tracks by horse, upon their substitution by the steam locomotive they nicknamed it the 'Iron Horse'.

I was proud to be a member of the haulage-chasing fraternity. We were a disparate collection of like-minded individuals from all parts of the country whose paths regularly crossed whilst in pursuit of our quarry – often during the increasingly frequent 'last' occasions. It was easy to sit by the lineside or visit steam sheds and either cop or photograph the steam locomotive. Haulage bashers, however, had the hardest job of all – catching their prey 'on the move'. It was the pre-Internet, Twitter and mobile phone age (present-day teenagers' jaws drop here!) and as such it was far more difficult and unpredictable to guarantee successful captures. The adrenalin rush and thrill of the chase cannot be replicated today. Knowing rather than hoping that a certain locomotive will put in an appearance somewhat defeats the sense of achievement when pre-planned junkets work out.

As the authorities gradually turned more and more services over to diesel we were obliged, because the remaining steam operated ones always only seemed to run during night hours, to lead a nomadic nocturnal existence – sometimes resulting in scenes of mayhem in the early hours whilst scrambling for the few seats available on mail/paper train services. The common denominator was haulage and whenever sighting each other information was exchanged. Did you know about such and such a train being steam operated? Had you heard about another being dieselised? There was without doubt much friendly rivalry amongst us. Often, when regaling (bragging even!) about our adventures, highlighting our own individual triumphs, there were always some participants silently cursing our good fortune – immediately making plans, usually to rectify their own shortfalls of red-lined entries (this referring to the locomotive listings being marked through within certain Ian Allan publications).

One by one the regions dispensed with steam. The WR in March 1966, the ER in May 1966, the ScR in May 1967, the SR in July 1967, the NER in November 1967 and finally the LMR in August 1968. What was on our side was the stamina of youth – a necessary requirement as, other than on my home patch of the SR, ALL journeys meant the minimum of at least one overnight spent on trains or in waiting rooms. As time progressed the itineraries became lengthier – my maximum British bash being of five nights without sleeping between clean sheets. Many lifelong friendships were formed. At the time we thought our hobby was heading for oblivion – little did we know that, courtesy of a dedicated band of enthusiasts and volunteers, hundreds of steam locomotives would be alive and well today. Indeed the railway preservation movement has become a burgeoning integral part of the tourism industry and is there for future generations to enjoy.

With the other regions of Britain having received my attention during the preceding two years, it wasn't until the April of 1966 that I made my first serious attempt at catching runs with steam locomotives allocated within the North Eastern Region (NER) of British Railways. Although the authorities had dieselised the majority of passenger services, there remained, predominantly in the West Riding, a pocket of secondary passenger services still assigned to steam power. I had almost left it too late but, as always in a race against time, likening the challenge to a gauntlet being thrown down, I set about locating and travelling with whatever remained.

I had deliberated titling the book *Tangerine Trails* alluding to, as older readers might recall, the distinctive sausage-shaped nameplate signs with white lettering on a tangerine background that adorned all the stations. With the regional timetable from the period also being contained within tangerine-coloured covers, the reader might have expected travel yarns from throughout the whole of North East England to be included. I therefore surmised that with just a handful of steam runs elsewhere *Riding Yorkshire's Final Steam Trains* was of greater linguistic correctness. Please join me as I detail the successes, disappointments, frustrations and joys of my self-appointed mission – which, while compiling, proved a therapeutic escape from today's 'must get there as fast as possible' rat race!

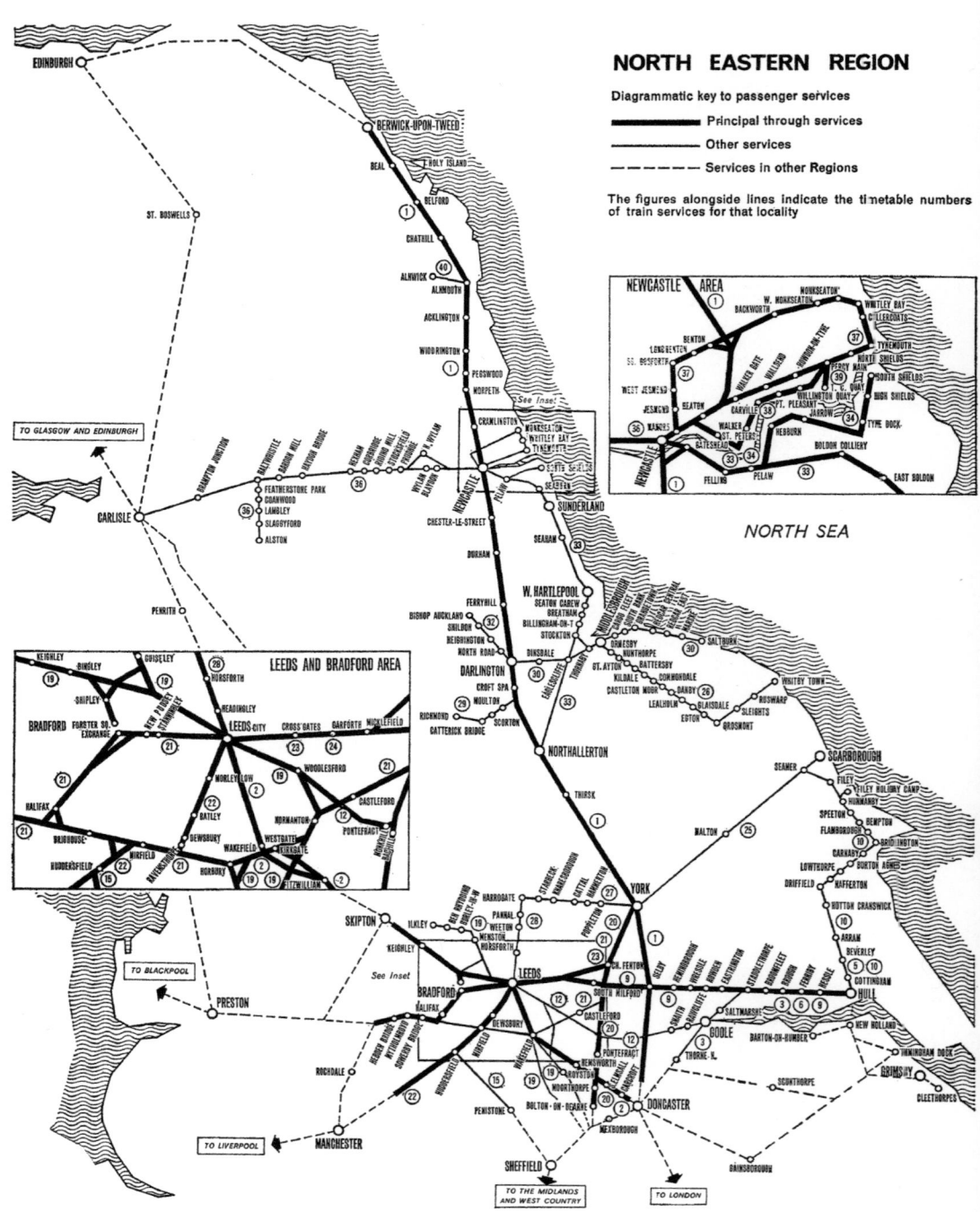

1966 NER system map.

1

Chasing: An Addiction Explained

TRAVELLING BY STEAM train has to be one of the greatest pleasures of life. The steam locomotive, a vital cog of the nineteenth-century industrial revolution, was undoubtedly one of man's finest achievements. Monopolising the movement of both passenger and freight traffic throughout the world for over a century it was only advancing technology in the form of electric- and diesel-powered alternatives that unseated it off from its throne. Unlike today's modern traction, which switches off and closes down upon a minor component failing, it usually got you home – even if it was itself ailing! Above all she was a living, breathing machine, often having a will of her own, but if treated with tender loving care would perform all that was demanded of her.

When frequently visiting some of the preserved railways, all the associated memories of my travelling years come back to me. The deafening exhaust echoing off of the cuttings and trees, the atmosphere, the heady nectar of grit, smoke and steam emanating from a living machine tackling a stiff gradient can only be truly appreciated by 'window hanging' out of the leading coach. It is beyond my comprehension how anyone can fail to be moved by the sight and sound of a steam locomotive hard at work. Personally, since first viewing them at Waterloo in the early '60s, I have had an ongoing love affair with them. It, or more universally referred to as she, has been a predominant mistress in my life for over half a century and, being the basis of this book, I defy the reader not to empathise as to the reason why I spent my formative years in pursuit of her.

Those of you who have read my previous tome on (steam) chasing, *The Great Steam Chase: The Last Days of Steam on BR's Southern Region*, can anticipate the brief of this explanatory chapter – slotted in here for the benefit of new readers. To set the scene as to when and where the seeds of my love of the Iron Horse were sown, I have to take the reader back to Waterloo – where I commenced my railway career. From my workplace, perched high up on the fourth floor, panoramic views of London were available if looking north, with just a massive expanse of the glass-covered roof if looking south. Although above the roof you could still hear all the station announcements and general noises from the activities below, the noisiest, emanating from the arrival (12–14) and departure (9–11) platforms, was of the steam-operated services.

Not initially an enthusiast when joining BR, it wasn't until mid '63 that any interest in disappearing steam and line closures finally fired sufficient interest to propel me out to places I had often directed prospective customers to in my job as telephone enquiry clerk. During my lunch break the 13 30 departure for Weymouth/Bournemouth West was often viewed from the end of platform 11 and perhaps it was the sheer majesty of the 8P Merchant Navy-class locomotive, with its safety valves lifting and the fireman fuelling the fire in readiness for the 143-mile journey ahead, that became the catalyst of a lifetime hobby. As I stood there, camera poised in readiness for the platform staff's whistle and the guard's 'right away' the potent power subsequently unleashed with the Pacific initially slipping (an inherent Bulleid weakness) on the greasy rail before finally finding her feet and powering the train into the distance must have sunk deep into the memory bank of an impressionable teenager.

At the rear of the train, ably assisting with an almighty shove, was the tank engine that had brought the stock in from Clapham Yard. Within the cavernous station train shed the ear-splitting cacophony of its thunderous exhaust sent the pigeons into orbit and made any conversation nigh on impossible. It all lasted for less than a minute before the tank engine driver slammed on the brakes to bring him to a stand alongside the ever-present gaggle of trainspotters always resident at the country end of platform 11. As I mentioned in my introduction, but I believe is worth restating, how anyone can fail to be impressed with the sight and sound of a steam locomotive in full flight is still beyond my comprehension. The intention of 'setting the scene' of my love of Iron Horse chasing has hopefully thus been achieved.

Having initially joined BR 'because my parents noted my interest in local timetables' (albeit bus!) I soon realised that the majority of the, certainly clerical, workforce not only saw their employment as a means to pay the mortgage but as an extension of their hobby – enhanced perhaps by the free and reduced rate travel facilities available! One particular friend, Bill, with whom I was to subsequently travel throughout Europe, often arrived in the office on a Monday morning with tales of his travels, photographs and timetables from all over the country. 'Get out there – use your travel facilities. It's all disappearing,' he often said. He was referring to the seemingly relentless number of routes closing as a consequence of Dr Beeching's axe (The Reshaping of British Railways, 1963) together with increasing dieselisation (Modernisation and Re-Equipment of the British Railways, 1955), the consequential outcome inevitably leading to the wholesale slaughter of the steam locomotive.

During the latter part of '63 curiosity began to get the better of me and I tentatively started to venture further afield, away from the mundane suburban commuter journeys undertaken so far, to routes (in the south of England) threatened with closure. During those early explorations I regrettably failed to document any facts and it was only by carrying a Brownie 127 camera and armed with an ever-deteriorating, flimsy paper network map on which I coloured in the relevant routes that any details survived the years. From the March of '64, however, having had a birthday present from my parents of a Kodak Colorsnap 35 and now always travelling with a notebook, the addiction was taking hold of me. This camera was equipped with the latest technology! It had a lens you could change to whatever the weather was doing i.e. bright sunshine, black-lined cloud or rain – not quite up to present-day equipment but adequate enough for my needs. Over the years, having been dropped, mislaid and cursed at (when the film jammed), it has provided me with over 1,000 images, some of which have found their way into the railway press. I wish I had taken more, but funds were directed at travel costs and, as a junior clerk, weren't always there.

As the months counted down towards the end of steam throughout Britain an ever-increasing number of enthusiasts could be witnessed on the scene. As mentioned in the introduction, rather than 'copping' a locomotive, we haulage bashers had to travel behind our quarry in order to redline the entry in our Ian Allan *Locoshed* books. The resulting satisfaction of seeing a page or column completed, perhaps even before our fellow conspirators, was without doubt what we all wanted to achieve. Being a haulage aficionado was undoubtedly a very self-appreciating variation of railway enthusiasm. No one else would benefit from our successes. Photographers can display their results for all to enjoy whereas what did I achieve – a book full of numbers! Memories, however, remain and whenever espying a photograph in a magazine or book of a train I might have travelled on, out come the notebooks and if indeed I was aboard the depicted train the relevant page gets extracted and stowed away in my 'I was there' folder.

Photography was always, as far as I was concerned, secondary to the pursuit of steam haulage – I would love to have been at the lineside as well, but being unable to be in both places at once a choice had to be made. It was a race against time. Success in tracking down steam-operated services came with experience, but it was always reassuring to see a wisp of smoke in the distance thus increasing the likelihood, but not always guaranteeing, the arrival of one. It was a mad, frenetic period – the camaraderie, the sense of urgency – knowing it would all end one day. Steam was disappearing at an extraordinarily fast rate, that fact alone providing the impetus to catch every potential movement. I sometimes wonder if had the steam locomotive not been dying so quickly whether such enthusiasm, such a fanatical chase, would have occurred.

Whilst appreciating the run-down conditions and constant failures, such a frequent occurrence towards the end, I still feel privileged to have witnessed the scenarios and participated in the pursuits with all their attendant emotional excitement and sadness. One of my friends from that period recently contacted me in connection with a previous book and, within the communication, highlighted how lucky we were to have enjoyed the scenarios, stating they were 'the best days of my life' – with which I concur. Whereas they were fun, providing excitement and joy for us enthusiasts to follow as a hobby, for the railway employees working with such run-down machines

My case and equipment. Everything I needed was crammed into this 16×10×4in attaché case.

in depots surrounded by dereliction and filth it was no joke. Their own employment was in doubt as steam sheds were closed down and I take my hat off to them for the chivalrous attitude they had towards us 'puffer nutters'.

Through all the travels contained within this tome my small attaché case (16×10×4in) went with me. All necessary equipment was contained within it: timetables, camera, Ian Allan books, notebooks, Lyons pies, Club biscuits, pens, flannel, handkerchief, stopwatch, cartons of orange drinks, sandwiches and, of course, a BR1 carriage key – a necessary piece of equipment to obtain a few hours sleep in vehicles stabled in the platforms/carriage sidings! Sturdy enough to sit on in crowded corridors of packed trains and doubling up as a pillow (albeit hard!) on overnight services it was in regular use through the final years of BR steam and even travelled with me throughout Europe in '68–69. Having survived many domestic upheavals over the years it now enjoys a comfortable retirement at the bottom of my 'railway cupboard' at home – containing all the documented travel information without which I could never have contemplated writing a book such as this.

As for apparel the anorak was not in existence then – to the best of my knowledge it was either a raincoat or a duffel coat with its attendant toggle fasteners. Usually, having commenced weekend travels directly after a day's work at the office, the obligatory tie (modern and straight edged) was always worn, albeit at peculiar angles after an overnight trip. The followers were classless. They came from all walks of life and included vicars, MPs (such as Robert Adley of Winchester who became a leading opponent to privatisation) and persons from many a varied employment. I often wondered how those who did not obtain cheap travel as an employment perk could afford it all – but then again ticket checks on trains were infrequent and there were no automatic barriers back then!

Upon returning home after each escapade, or within a few days if very late back, all the necessary details collected were transferred into legibility within large A4-sized desk diaries. Separate small books kept individual locomotive mileages, shed visits and timed trains. I lost the pre-June-1965 notebooks from which I extracted the information but have retained all the rest. There was much to do. Each 'capture' was redlined in the Ian Allan *Locoshed* book – more often than not being surrounded by blacked-out entries indicating sister locomotives having been withdrawn! These books were reissued quite regularly and, with the continuous transferring around of locomotives (information updated courtesy of *Railway World* magazine) resulting from line/depot closures, much midnight oil was burnt in just attempting to keep it all current. Luckily the detailing of such minutiae came easy to me through my work as a BR train planner where precise and accurate documentation was a requirement. Then there was a surprising educational side benefit as regards the named locomotives. Reference to library books or encyclopedias were often made as to who was *Sir Harry Hinchcliffe* or *Clive of India*, where is *Bihar and Orissa*, what was *Bellerophon*. It was much more difficult back then, not having the ability to type in the search box on your handheld iPhone! So off we go ...

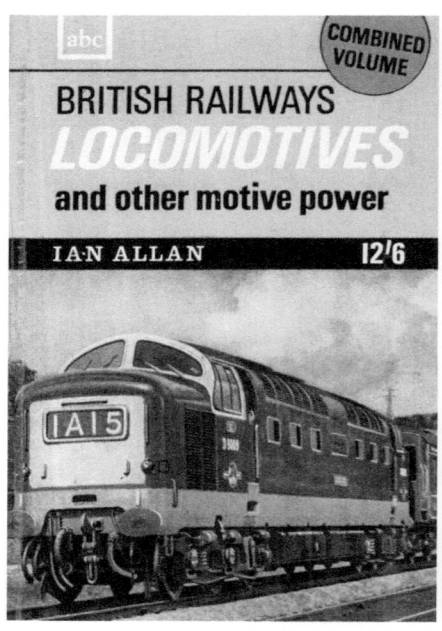

Front cover of the Autumn '64 *Ian Allan Combined Volume*. (Ian Allan)

Front cover of Part 2 of an Ian Allan *ABC*. (Ian Allan)

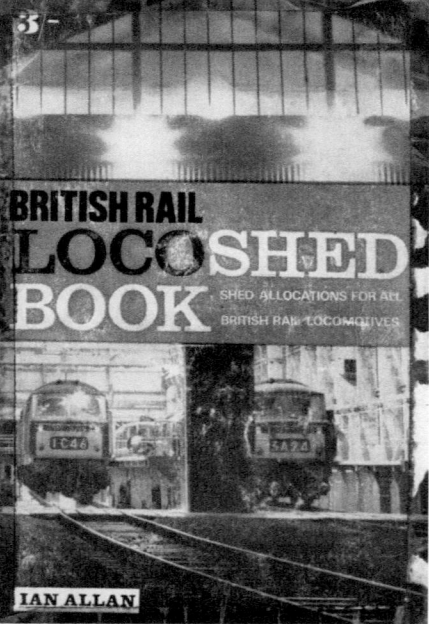

The *Locoshed* books issued by Ian Allan were an essential tool in keeping up to date with the whereabouts and numbers of steam locomotives. Here are the front covers of two issues: Autumn 1966 (left) and Autumn 1967 (right). (Ian Allan)

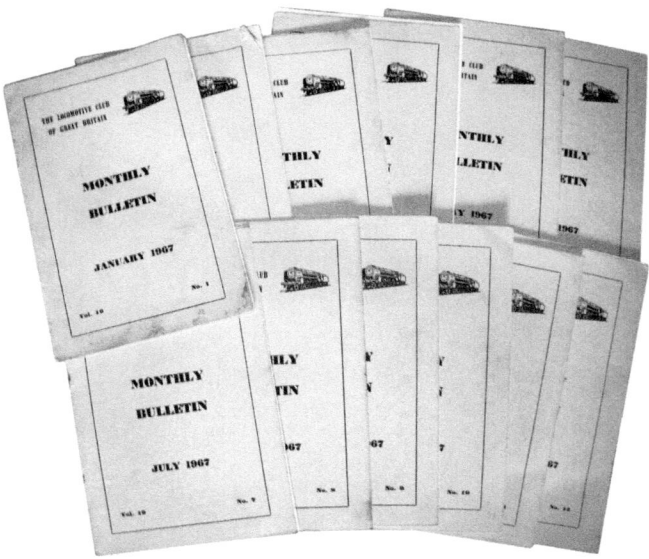

The twelve issues of the 1967 *LCGB Bulletin*. These small monthly publications provided both the information to alter the *Locoshed Book* entries plus reports from all the regions by members in respect of which trains were steam operated, shed closures and their own rail tours. (The Locomotive Club of Great Britain)

The twelve issues of the 1966 *Railway World* magazines. It was the reading of 'the office copy' in those early years of railway employment, with photographs and articles of railway routes about to be axed by the good doctor, that inspired me to travel over them before it was too late. (Ian Allan)

2

A SOUTHERNER VENTURES 'ABROAD'

NORTH EAST ENGLAND was the cradle of the railways. The world's first public railway to use steam locomotives was the 25-mile-long Stockton & Darlington Railway over which, in September 1825, George Stephenson's *Locomotion No. 1* worked the inaugural train. Primarily concerned with the faster movement of coal, the need for an alternative mode of transportation other than the horse-drawn method available until then had led to a myriad of railway lines being constructed throughout the coalfields of Durham and Northumberland. Always on the lookout for profiteering on behalf of their shareholders, passenger traffic, until then of secondary importance, became a valuable source of income to the railway companies of which the North Eastern Railway (NER) (1854–1922), resulting from numerous amalgamations over the preceding years, became the main player. Few railways achieved such regional domination and, given the level of rivalry that existed in much less fertile regions for railway operation, the NER was fortunate in not facing greater competition.

In the sixty-eight years of the NER's existence the railway expanded from a route mileage of 700 to 4,900. It bequeathed to the London & North Eastern Railway (LNER) (1923–1947) a significant portion of the East Coast Main Line (ECML), some of the finest stations in the country, e.g.York, Darlington, Hull and Newcastle, an electrified suburban system at Newcastle and massive freight traffic. Little changed upon the 1923 grouping or indeed after the 1948 nationalisation. The railways carried on as always, moving both freight and passenger traffic in abundance. They, together with their British Road Services arm, had the monopoly. There were no motorways and car ownership was only for the well off. Change, however, was on the horizon. Post-war affluence, allowing family car ownership to become the norm, together with continual increases in permitted weight limits for lorries, was to challenge the railways' monopoly on all fronts. With the loss of many of the traditional heavy industries over the years, coupled with the 1955 British Railways (BR) Modernisation plan envisaging the elimination of steam traction by 1968, the steam locomotive, the main thrust of my hobby, was heading for oblivion. My interests therefore morphed from that of a line basher into the chasing of the Iron Horse itself. There was little time left!

The date was August 1964 and within a few weeks the *Daily Herald* would cease publication and be superseded by what has become Britain's largest-circulation paper, *The Sun*. Musically it was a great period to live through with *Top of the Pops* and Radio Luxembourg belting out hits from groups such as the Beatles, the Rolling Stones and the Animals – Manfred Mann's *Do Wah Diddy Diddy* sitting at the number-one spot during the last two weeks of that August.

Although having travelled on overnight services to the West of England during the previous month, the familiarity of destinations already known both from having holidayed there over the years with my parents and my Southern Region (SR) telephone enquiry job, voyaging north that August night it seemed I was venturing into the unknown. Sure I had studied maps, viewed photographs and read timetables as regards the cities and towns I was to visit, but nothing broadens the mind like actually travelling there in person. Strange dialects, unusual-sounding destinations – it all caused an adolescent 17-year-old some consternation determining if I was on the correct train/platform to ensure my plans were adhered to. The overnight service down the ECML, specifically advertised for Geordies working away during the week to visit home with cheap tickets, was chock-a-block. This service called at all main stations, and the consequential passage through the open-plan carriages of people looking for non-existent seats resulted in very little shut-eye being obtained en route.

Newcastle station was, and remains, an impressive testimonial to the Victorian engineer John Dobson. Opened in 1850 by Queen Victoria, it was a joint enterprise between the York, Newcastle and Berwick and the Newcastle and Carlisle railways. The station's train shed has a distinctive barrel-vaulted roof with three curved arched spans – the first example of its kind – which set the 'house style' for the NER's subsequent main-line stations. If approached from the south you cross over a high-level Robert Stephenson-designed bridge straddling the River Tyne while at the north end was once a complex diamond-crossing-equipped rail junction, which the succeeding NER claimed to be the largest in the world. As is so common these days, the operational part of the station has been significantly reduced and much of the superfluous space converted to provide additional car parking. Back in 1964, glad of the opportunity to stretch my legs, I positioned myself at the north end of the station viewing the aforementioned diamond crossing being much utilised by a plethora of steam locomotive classes only previously read about in *The Observer's Book of Railway Locomotives of Britain*.

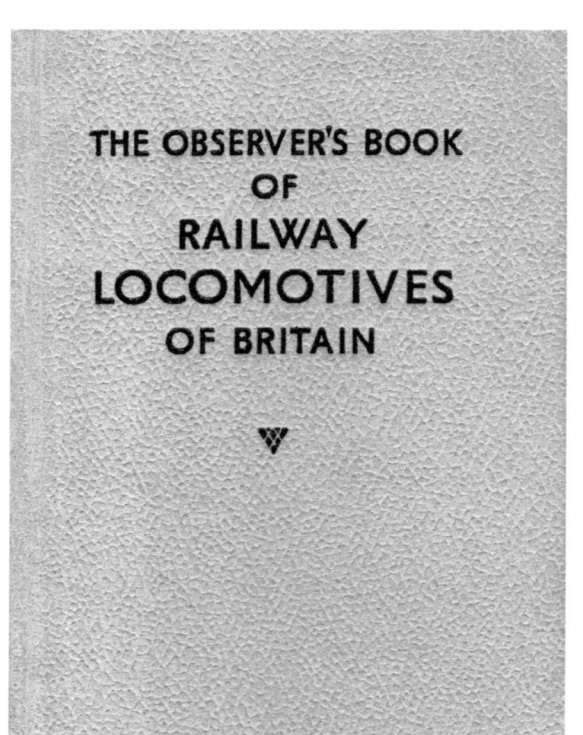

Front cover of *The Observer's Book of Railway Locomotives of Britain* given to me as a Christmas present in 1963.

The next seven photographs were all taken from Newcastle station platforms between 6 a.m. and 8 a.m. on Saturday 22 August 1964. I had never witnessed any of these classes before – having only seen photographs of them in magazines and books such as *The Observer's Book of Railway Locomotives of Britain*. Entering the station at the north end is one of the 206 Stanier-designed LMS 4MT 2-6-4Ts, 42548, this 28-year-old example having been built by North British (Glasgow). She was a long way from her Newton Heath (Manchester) home and was withdrawn from Birkenhead in February 1967.

A Southerner Ventures 'Abroad'

Easing her way past on the goods lines is one of the seventy-eight Gresley-designed 4-6-2 A3s – LNER 60080 *Dick Turpin*. Built in 1924 by North British, she had been displaced from the crack ECML expresses by diesels and was to be withdrawn from her Gateshead home two months later.

Sister A3, 60112 *St Simon*, is seen being watered having taken over the 01 00 Kings Cross to Edinburgh at Newcastle. This 41-year-old New England (Peterborough) allocated 7P Pacific was withdrawn at the end of that year. With more self-confidence I would have changed plans and taken the opportunity to ride with her the 114 miles to Edinburgh.

One of Gresley's 184 powerful LNER 6MT 2-6-2 V2s storms through on the goods lines with a northbound freight. Built at Darlington in 1943, Gateshead allocated 60976 became one of the fortunate few surviving into 1966 – being withdrawn in the October of that year at St Margarets (Edinburgh).

Blyth allocated 44-year-old LNER Q6 0-8-0 63413 works a southbound freight tender first. A total of 120 of these Raven-designed locomotives were built, this one at Armstrong Whitworth (Newcastle), between 1913 and 1921 – 63413 ending her days at Tyne Dock in January 1967.

Seventy examples of the ninety-two-strong LNER V1 4MT 2-6-2T class were given higher-pressure boilers and reclassified V3 – one of which, 67646, reposes at Newcastle station awaiting her next call of duty. By this date a mere eight remained – 67646 being withdrawn from her home depot of Gateshead three months later.

A poorly positioned photograph but included as my only shot of an active Worsdell/Raven LNER 5F 0-6-0 J27! A total of 115 of these 0-6-0s were built – Blyth-allocated 65882 becoming one of the final five being withdrawn at Sunderland in September 1967.

On the goods lines, representatives of Q6 0-8-0, J27 0-6-0, V2 2-6-2 and V3 2-6-2T classes were noted while in the station A3 Pacific 60112 *St Simon* took the 01 00 ex-Kings Cross forward to Edinburgh. In years to come I would have changed plans and taken the opportunity to ride with her the 114 miles to Edinburgh, but lacking the self-confidence in my ability to vary from my planned itinerary, I let her go. It was an opportunity lost. I had been advised, by those more knowledgeable than I, that Preston was a mecca for steam activity and so, the two hours spent at Newcastle having passed by very quickly, I made my way there via Carlisle and, being a somewhat angst-ridden youth far away from home, located and stayed in B&B accommodation close by the station – my first ever night on my own. That was the only occasion I slept between clean sheets while chasing steam-hauled services in Britain. The lure of unusual workings over routes which in daytime used DMUs but at night had steam-operated services proved too invaluable to miss out on.

3

PLANNING THE ATTACK

HAVING PRIMARILY HOMED in on my resident (Southern) region's steam passenger services during 1964, during the following year I began to widen my coverage to services elsewhere in Britain. Several trips were made to Scotland – the first being in May and calculatingly scheduled to travel over the Port Road between Dumfries and Stranraer prior to its closure the following month. Continuing on to other steam services in Scotland that day I passed through the North Eastern Region en route home. The train concerned, the 20 20 Edinburgh Waverley to Kings Cross, had one of the diesel locomotives (DLs) that had replaced ECML steam three years earlier, English Electric Type 5 Deltic D9001 *St Paddy*, at the helm. All other Scottish visits that year, the Indian summer of the displaced LNER Gresley A4s on the Glasgow/Aberdeen services, were made via the then still steam-infested West Coast Main Line (WCML).

Roger Price's publications, which he produced himself with all proceeds going to the SR Orphanage at Woking, kickstarted my interest in the NER.

The front cover of the North Eastern Region timetable for the summer of 1966 – often referred to throughout this book as the 'tangerine bible'.

Effectively unaware of the many, albeit short-haul, steam passenger services remaining in this hitherto unexplored part of Britain (Yorkshire), it was by purchasing, at the cost of 1s 6d (7½p), one of colleague Roger Price's pamphlets that I unearthed what became a pleasing diversity of steam classes never witnessed before at work. Having recently met Roger, I asked him where he obtained the information to compile his publications. His reply was that he had written to all the regions who, upon learning that any profits were for the railway children's orphanage, willingly listed the remaining steam-hauled passenger services for him.

A new untapped area of steam locomotive catches was the indispensable nectar obligatory for a haulage basher such as myself. So what was there to discover? The crack express services over the ECML from Kings Cross to Leeds, Newcastle and Edinburgh had long gone Deltic, the Trans-Pennine trains had succumbed to either Peak or Brush DLs and although the majority of secondary passenger services had become DMUs there still remained, if details received to hand were accurate, a sufficient number of trains justifying investigation. The only two NER-allocated steam locomotives I'd had runs with prior to 1966 were both Holbeck (Leeds) allocated, they being Black 5 45211 and Jubilee 45593 *Kolhapur*. The former had been purloined by the Colwick foreman for the 17 15 Nottingham Victoria/Marylebone one day during February '66 and *Kolhapur* was caught into Carlisle during August '65 while returning from a Scottish bash. So there was plenty to go for.

More hard-earned wages were spent purchasing at 2s 0d (10p) a copy of the North Eastern Region public timetable which became my *Tangerine Bible*, in which I proceeded to mark the train services depicted as steam powered with a red line through the centre of the timings column. It was a more problematic task than encountered when locating similar services within the corresponding green Southern Region timetable. The reason was twofold: firstly there were no internal 'working' publications available to me as there had been (for SR services) in the offices where I worked at Waterloo, and secondly my lack of in-depth knowledge with regard to sheds, train services and geography. Nevertheless, over a period of weeks during the dark winter evenings of early February '66 (when not chasing Bulleids), I took up the challenge.

Proceeding alphabetically, the first entry I came across was the Barnsley departure at 06 10 for Wakefield Kirkgate. Initially perplexed about how to access this train, when reaching the letter 'W' I realised it was the return working of an 05 15 ex-Wakefield and, as was often the case, the only non-DMU working over the line. Next we come to Bradford Exchange – which showed four departures per day for Leeds Central and three for Wakefield Westgate. Two other once-daily oddities were the 15 20 for Stockport and 22 00 for Huddersfield. The other Bradford station, Forster Square, was shown to have ten departures for Leeds City. This was more like it. I surmised that by positioning myself at a location such as Bradford I could come and go as choices dictated – although, taking into account the short distances involved, the likelihood of catching the same locomotive on several occasions throughout the day was always going to be a possibility.

Moving on alphabetically we come to Halifax and an 04 38 for Manchester, which was shown as a 5MT provided by 12A MO and 9D MX locomotive (all shed codes are listed in Appendix IV). This train, I was to discover, turned out to be the 02 10 York to Manchester Victoria Calder Valley mail train – a service, which as the reader will come to appreciate, I was to become a frequent user of. The other departure from Halifax each day was the 08 48 for Wakefield Westgate – a somewhat circuitously routed portion (via Huddersfield and Wakefield Kirkgate) eventually destined for Kings Cross.

Harrogate had an isolated 11 40 for Leeds Central each day, but now we come to the two Leeds stations. Leeds City had nine departures for Bradford Forster Square and six for Carnforth/Morecambe Promenade. As if that wasn't enough, the nearby Leeds Central had four departures for Bradford Exchange, one for Halifax and what had become the final steam penetration into the diesel desert of Eastern Region, the 16 45 for Doncaster. Normanton had an 04 25 departure for Rochdale and an 07 06 for York (04 20 ex-Manchester).

Sheffield Midland had two Leeds City departures at 02 00 and 07 06 and a York at 08 10. The depicted power for all of these services was either a 4MTT or 5MT. Not known at the time but revealed in research for this book was that although there were eighteen LNER B1s shared between Wakefield and Low Moor depots, if Roger's publication was to prove accurate, none were booked to perform passenger work – any 5MT duties shown being booked for Holbeck's Black 5s. Similarly, with nothing indicating 6P operated then, the ten Jubilees were also seemingly inaccessible to haulage enthusiasts. So with all that information to hand I then spent more hours pouring over the *Tangerine Bible* planning a comprehensive itinerary for my visit at the end of March in an attempt to travel on the maximum number of those workings. One thing was certain: the ability to make any visit to this area of Britain worthwhile was of course to travel there overnight. This not only eliminated any costs associated with B&Bs but also enabled travel on (very) early morning services, which, I was to find out, were most beneficial to a steam chaser.

4

HERE WE GO

PERHAPS IT IS opportune, prior to embarking, to briefly summarise the geographical scene at the time of my travels. West Riding was one of three historic subdivisions of Yorkshire. Unlike most English counties that were divided into hundreds, Yorkshire, being so large, was divided first into *thrithjungar* (an old Norse word meaning 'third parts') that were called the three Ridings (East, West and North) and later the City of York, which lay within the city walls and was not part of any Riding. The majority of my travels in this book were within the administrative county, County of York – West Riding (1889–1974) – the larger conurbations of Bradford, Leeds, Huddersfield, Halifax and Sheffield having their own municipal boroughs. Local government reorganisation in 1974 saw the abolition of the Ridings and Yorkshire was devolved between a number of metropolitan and non-metropolitan counties.

The time had arrived to put those hours of planning into action. I had chosen Wednesday 30 March (1966) and at 19 years of age not being old enough to vote (it was reduced to 18 four years later) in that day's General Election didn't delay my departure, having briefly visited home after work. Harold Wilson's Labour Government had increased its majority from the previous election held a mere seventeen months earlier from five (which had been reduced to one resulting from by-election defeats) to ninety-six. That month had also seen a great many protest marches throughout the USA against involvement in the Vietnam War while back here Pickles the dog had recovered the stolen World Cup trophy wrapped in newspaper in a South London garden and Beatle John Lennon had made his infamous 'we are more popular than Jesus' remark.

The Walker Brothers' *The Sun Ain't Gonna Shine Anymore*, holding the number-one spot for four weeks, seemed somewhat prophetic as the weather was cold and, as I was to discover later in the trip, deteriorating rapidly. Putting all that to one side the plan was to survive on the railway system for four consecutive nights – my lengthiest voyage into the unknown to date. Was I going to succumb to sleep without warning – missing stations I should have alighted at? Would I have the stamina to last the course or have to return home earlier than anticipated with my tail between my legs – foregoing the completion of my itinerary? All these questions are what concerned parents worry about and mine were no exception. These concerns, however daunting, were far from my mind as the adrenalin and excitement of the possibilities that awaited me foreshadowed any apprehensions I might have had. The prime motivation for this bash was the London Midland Region (LMR) timetable changes, heralding a considerable reduction in steam-powered passenger services, coming into operation just weeks later – the NER section being a twenty-four-hour 'taster'.

I headed north that night out of the building site of Euston (it was being redeveloped in connection with the WCML electrification – the historic Doric arch being a notable casualty) on the 22 35 sleeper departure for the Cumbrian coast resort of Whitehaven. This nine-hour train journey was one of the casualties of the timetable change and was the sole surviving passenger service over the Cumberland coastline north of Barrow with steam. Changing at Whitehaven onto a DMU for the short distance to Workington after a shed bash I continued on over the doomed scenic Lake District line (closed three weeks later) via Cockermouth and Keswick to Carlisle. Because of its strategic location, Carlisle was made a key station by the Romans who established it to serve the forts on their coast-to-coast Hadrian's Wall, and although visiting it on many occasions during the final years of steam this day was the only occasion I ventured out of the station. Guided by my ever-present Ian Allan's *British Locomotive Shed Directory,* a publication constantly referred to in order to access sheds and cross cities, a visit to both sheds at Carlisle (Kingmoor and Upperby) was undertaken during the six hours there.

I have documentary proof of my visits, i.e. cops at both sheds but only photographs from Upperby – perhaps, with no permits for either shed, the Kingmoor foreman was less approachable. A tired and weary gricer* then boarded the 16 37 departure from Carlisle for Bradford. This 105-mile stopping service via Appleby and Skipton had become, together with the 15 40 opposite way working, the last all-year booked steam-operated train over the MR route to Yorkshire. The three-coach train had Kingmoor's Black 5 45254 in charge rather than an expected Brit, the near four-hour journey calling at all the short-platformed, dimly lit stations high in the Pennines. In the gathering gloom with worsening weather conditions (in the form of thickening persistent falling snow) it somehow heightened the sense of adventure not known outside my usual home territory of the SR – night-time journeys there often accompanied by the reassuring glow of lights from the frequently passing EMUs. Nostalgia was provided

---

* The word 'gricer' was one of the more printable pseudonyms accredited to us enthusiasts. I have uncovered two theories as to its origin. You can either believe that it emanated from trainspotter Richard Grice, who became legendary for travelling the entire BR network, or from two Manchester Locomotive Society members on holiday on the Durham moors who, having 'copped' two grouse, termed the word grice as being the plural of grouse. The comparison (between the animals and enthusiasts) is that, to the casual observer, they appear to be 'wondering around aimlessly' – in the latter case their habitat being station platforms! You choose.

for me courtesy of the short-wheelbase London Midland & Scottish (LMS) carriages with steam heating seeping from every possible orifice throughout the train.

The topography of the line (described in Chapter 9) was far from my thoughts that bitterly cold night. When planning this trip I hadn't taken into consideration any climatic variations and was becoming slightly concerned as to how I was to keep warm over the next sixty-odd hours, particularly at night. I reasoned that most of the time I would be on trains and, back then, waiting rooms at main-line stations were always open, albeit often without heating. After a surprisingly on-time arrival into Bradford Forster Square station, an hour's fester resulted, disappointingly, in the same locomotive, having been turned and serviced at the nearby Manningham shed, returning to work the 13½ miles to Leeds on the 21 30 departure for St Pancras. Unlike nowadays when Forster Square dispatches only local services, back then you could catch trains for Birmingham, Devon, Carlisle and, as the case that night, London St Pancras. After a short half-hour journey the vista of Leeds, the once great seat of the clothing trade, was upon me.

The present day Leeds City station started life in 1869, initially called New Station, as a joint enterprise between the London & North Western Railway (LNWR) and NER. Situated at the end of a mile-long connection carried entirely on viaducts and bridges the twelve-platformed station itself was partially built over the River Aire. Resulting from rationalisation in 1938 involving the closure of the adjacent Wellington Street station, it was renamed Leeds City. In 1967, in connection with the closure of Leeds Central, which encompassed the replacement of the 100-year-old bridges over the Leeds and Liverpool Canal, the opportunity was taken to construct a new concourse and, bucking the trend, build an overall roof. In 2002 a further rebuilding project took place with the construction of additional approach tracks and an increase to seventeen platforms. A recent government authorisation (2013) of a new southern entrance spanning the River Aire certainly vindicates the station's hierarchy as being the third busiest (after Glasgow Central and Birmingham New Street) outside London.

Back to 1966 and on that evening's journey I stayed aboard the train from Bradford – the delights of protracted waiting time there being deferred to the early hours of the following morning. The train had reversed and was taken forward from Leeds by Peak D84. This diesel was an example of the 173-strong Sulzer Type 4 class which, because the first ten were named after mountains, became known to all as Peaks. Over recent years they had displaced steam over former MR routes between St Pancras/Bristol to Derby and the North East. Travelling south to Sheffield, I was captivated by scenes I had never viewed before – passing en route through the industrial heartland of Britain. The night sky seemed ablaze, this illusion being caused by the reflection from the many furnaces at steel mills adjacent to the line. Together with power stations emitting vast clouds of dirty smoke the panorama viewed on the journey was completely alien to a 'southerner'.

Sheffield, situated at the confluence of rivers Don and Sheaf, is renowned throughout the world for its production of cutlery, made from locally manufactured steel back then but nowadays more reliant on cheaper imports from Sweden. Another, perhaps less well-known, event at Sheffield is that it is where the World Snooker Championships are held each year at the Crucible Theatre. There is a standing joke among railway-orientated snooker fans that to access a colour you had to get past a red – a reference to Sheffield signalmen's regular delaying tactics for all trains approaching the station!

Sheffield Midland station, opened in 1870, was the fifth and last station built in the city centre. Expanded in 1905 with two extra platforms and new frontage, Second World War damage put the roofs beyond economic repair and they were eventually removed in 1956 and replaced with utilitarian low-level awnings.

In 1970 Sheffield's other main station, Victoria, closed and the remaining Penistone-routed services were diverted there. I had travelled here that night to catch what was indicated in Roger's book as being a steam-operated service, the 02 00 departure for Leeds. It was a two-hour wait and while the waiting room had a coal fire it didn't appear to have any effect on my numb body – the welcome sight of one of Holbeck's Black 5s, 45204, bringing the stock in half an hour before departure answering my prayers. Unfortunately it was only a temporary respite from the cold and once more, after a 03 30 arrival into the draughty funnel they call Leeds City, further body-chilling temperatures were endured. Unlike stations such as Crewe and Carlisle, where a great many periods were to be spent during the early hours over the next few years, Leeds City was devoid of any all-night refreshment room, and although the station had a waiting room it was located adjacent to the concourse, well away from the platforms. That was no good for an enthusiast – you had to be positioned where the trains were running should something unusual, e.g. steam vice diesel, turn up. No gain without pain – when daybreak arrives it will all have been worth it I tried to convince myself.

With daybreak arriving and having supped a cup of tea and devoured some compressed day-old sandwiches for sustenance, it was with a mix of apprehension and excitement that I was about to head for pastures new. I was tired and although Peak diesel D33 working the 05 58 departure, the overnight St Pancras/Bradford Forster Square, offered some respite from the cold I was somewhat concerned that many steam services may have already succumbed to increased use of the many newly delivered Type 2 Sulzer diesels frequently seen in the area. Eventually totalling nearly 500, these machines were referred to by steam followers at the time as 'Splutterbugs' because of their rasping erratic exhaust – younger enthusiasts, however, have awarded them the nickname 'Rats' as they were perceived to have overrun certain parts of BR (the Scottish equivalents being 'Mac Rats'!).

Over to Bradford's Forster Square station and another small history lesson is due. The first station at Bradford was sited close to this location and opened by the Leeds and Bradford Railway in July 1846. After the Midland Railway swallowed up this small independent concern seven years later, the station was rebuilt only for it to be once again redeveloped in 1890 with six platforms, an overall glazed roof and an accompanying hotel. In 1924, after the spacious gardens with its statue of the nineteenth-century politician William Edward Forster were opened nearby, the station gained its present name of Forster Square. Nothing much changed until the 1960s when, similar to Sheffield, the overall roof was replaced by utilitarian 'butterfly' awnings. The line in from Shipley was truncated in 1990 when a new three-platformed station, electrified in 1994, was built on the western side of the former station. The old station was later demolished to make way for the Broadgate shopping centre, which, resulting from the early '90s recession, was never constructed, the site initially used as a car park prior to the present tax office being built there. Part of the screen arcade that fronted the 1890 station, together with the Midland Hotel, remains, becoming, in 2005, much more visible, when the city centre redevelopment began and Forster House was demolished.

Returning to that cold morning in March, rescue (from a possible succession of diesels) came in the form of Manningham's Fairburn 42093 on the 07 30 Forster Square departure for London. Having taken this service through to Leeds, the sparsity of trains meant I was unable to return to Bradford for the following 08 50 departure, causing me to alight short on a returning Bradford service at the intermediate triangular platformed station of Shipley – waiting over half an hour for what turned out to be her now-preserved sister 42085. So far so good. Noting that just one train per day out of Harrogate was red-lined in my timetable as being steam operated, I travelled the 18¼ miles there for, respectively, the catch of the day – in the form of York-allocated B1 61199. She was working the 11 40 'portion' from Harrogate to Leeds Central en route to London Kings Cross. That year's timetable changes, which were to inflict so much disappointment during the follow-up bash two months later, saw the cessation of steam on this Harrogate train. My time within North Eastern Region was coming to an end because, as previously mentioned, the WCML services were to undergo a dramatic reduction in steam workings within weeks and I was off over there later that day. There were, however, several more services to investigate. These were the Leeds/Bradford to Carnforth/Morecambe via Skipton services – destined for dieselisation within weeks. For the next few hours I station-hopped between Leeds/Bingley/Skipton and Hellifield – catching runs with four different Black 5s, two of which were from the soon-to-be-closed Lancaster Green Ayre shed. A bonus caught up in all this was Kingmoor's Brit 70040 *Clive of India* on the balancing train to yesterday's all-station stopper over Ais Gill – the 15 40 Bradford Forster Square to Carlisle. So I went on my way to the LMR – the following day's chaotic running and snow-blocked Shap being another story! Summing up my first visit to the NER – in just twenty-four hours I had caught ten locomotives from four different classes through areas never travelled before. It had all the potential of many new haulages and I vowed to return as soon as funds would allow.

5

THE LAST REMAINING OUTPOSTS

HAVING MADE A stab at obtaining runs with steam in the NER area, perhaps now is the time to summarise what was available to me. Before delving into the matter the reader has to appreciate that all the information contained within both this and the following chapter has been unearthed whilst undertaking extensive research for this book, i.e. was not known about at the time. It was only by updating my Ian Allan *Locoshed Book* months after events had occurred (i.e. which sheds had closed to steam or which locomotives had been withdrawn or transferred away to freight only locations) that I had any hope of keeping abreast of the continually fluctuating steam scene. As for real-time visits to the area it was very much hit and miss. Surprising appearances by locomotives I had listed as belonging far away, together with services not known to have been dieselised, led to extraordinary highs and lows in a chaser's life. By the April of 1966 only seven Motive Power Depots (MPDs) remained that had booked steam passenger work and a brief summary of their allocations now follows:

Tweedmouth (52D), located on the ECML just south of the Scottish border, was responsible for the provision of power, out-stabled at the sub shed of Alnmouth 32 miles to the south for the few remaining steam duties on the 3-mile Alnwick branch. Both Tweedmouth and Alnwick closed to steam in June 1966.

Leeds Holbeck (55A) was located about half a mile south of Leeds City station. It was responsible for the remaining steam-operated services out of both Leeds stations to Morecambe (shared with LMR sheds), Harrogate, Sheffield and Doncaster. It was the shed's provision, during their Indian summer of '66, of their Jubilees for the three Scottish services via Ais Gill each Saturday that is best remembered. The shed, with its half-dozen LMS tanks, also shared responsibility with Manningham/Low Moor for the Bradford portions to both Forster Square and Bradford Exchange – its stud of eighteen Black 5s, however, standing in for any shortfall. Often providing replacement steam power for rescuing trains on the Trans-Pennine services when the Peak/Brush Type 4 DLs got into trouble, the shed also serviced the many LMR steam incursions into the area. After the cull in October 1967 (when *officially* 55A closed to steam!) just two Jubilees, 45562 *Alberta* and 45593 *Kolhapur*, together with K1 62005 were kept on the books – ostensibly for rail tours and/or preservation. The remaining months of 1967 saw Holbeck continue to deal with steam incursions from the LMR together with the regular 17 47 FO Manchester Exchange and 23 38 SuO Liverpool Lime Street locomotives. Into 1968 and, against all odds, the 03 32 Leeds to Halifax (for Manchester) remained steam powered, in the form of a Newton Heath Black 5 until that May.

Farnley Junction (55C) shed was located on the former LNWR route 2 miles south of Leeds at which an alternative route to Huddersfield via Cleckheaton and Heckmondwike diverged. The shed had an allocation of just three Jubilees and five Black 5s for passenger traffic. With the shed's closure on 23 November 1966 the two remaining Jubilees (*Sturdee* having been withdrawn in August) and three of the Black 5s were transferred to Holbeck – the balance going to the freight depot of Stourton.

Normanton (55E) shed was perhaps one of the more viewable sheds. Situated just north of the station itself, the majority of occupants could easily be seen from passing trains. Most of its workload was freight orientated – the only two passenger departures it had to provide for being the 04 25 for Rochdale and the 07 06 for York (04 20 ex-Manchester). An LMR-allocated Black 5 worked the latter train to Normanton from where, judging from the variety of power provided, it seemed to cause the foreman a headache. Anything from LMS tanks/Flying Pigs/Black 5s to LNER B1s were sent out for the 24½-mile onward journey to York. Until March 1967 only two passenger locomotives (Fairburns 42083 and 42149) were on the shed's books. After that date, resulting from displacement elsewhere, the allocation swelled, peaking in July 1967, to eight tanks and five Black 5s – all being condemned in that October's NER cull. Steam servicing facilities were kept, however, for visiting LMR-based locomotives until the shed's closure (to steam) in January 1968.

Bradford Manningham (55F) shed was located 1¼ miles north of Bradford Forster Square adjacent to Manningham station (closed 1965), on the Midland Railway (MR) route to Shipley. All locomotives working into Forster Square were serviced there and its own allocation of seven LMS Fairburn tanks only ever worked the 13½ miles to and from Leeds City, with the portions of services originating from or destined for Birmingham/Devon/St Pancras. Upon closure on 29 April 1967, resulting from service alterations involving Leeds Central's demise, three went to Normanton and three to Wakefield – 42052 being withdrawn.

Wakefield (56A) was a lengthy twenty-minute walk from Kirkgate station and was primarily a freight depot with over 100 of the War Department (WD) Austerity 2-8-0s allocated there for the intensive coal traffic. Never possessing more than seven LMS tanks and ten LNER B1s, the few passenger services out of Kirkgate and the Westgate/Bradford portions (the latter shared with Low Moor) were always liable for a 56A locomotive. Wakefield's two Jubilees *Bellerophon* and *Ulster* were both withdrawn in January of 1967 being replaced by two Black 5s. The shed closed on 3 June 1967.

Bradford Low Moor (56F) was located adjacent to Low Moor station 3 miles south of Bradford Exchange. Although the station closed in 1965, a proposal involving a budget of £10 million will see it reopen as part of a metro system – December 2015 being mooted at the time of writing. Low Moor's allocation of LMS tanks varied in numbers between 7 and 10 – withdrawals being supplanted by a cavalcade of displaced examples from Tebay, Trafford Park and Birkenhead. Their one Jubilee, 45565 *Victoria*, was kept in spotless condition as befitted a depot 'favourite', but alas went to the cutters torch in January 1967. There had always been a small stud of Black 5s at Low Moor (never exceeding four over the final year) with incoming transfers from closing depots replacing withdrawals. The seven B1s gradually dwindled in numbers until extinction in December 1966 only for a surprise transfer in of three during August '67 (the month the shed was recoded 55J). The immaculately turned out, and subsequently preserved, B1 61306 hauled *The Yorkshire Pullman* on Saturday 30 September 1967 and pre-empted the depot's provision of a suitably adorned 42152 on the final day of steam on the Sunday – the depot closing at midnight.

6

THE MAIN PLAYERS

ALTHOUGH BRIEFLY MENTIONED in the preceding chapter when detailing which sheds were still providing steam power for passenger services operating during the final months of steam in the NER, here I offer greater detail of the six different classes which were liable to be sent out by the foreman.

LMS Stanier Tanks
Designed by W. Stanier, 206 of these 4MT 2-6-4 tanks were constructed between 1935 and 1943 at Derby and North British (Glasgow) works. Based on his predecessor Fowler's 2-6-4Ts they were initially allocated throughout the London, Tilbury & Southend (LT&S) system for use on the extensive passenger services into Fenchurch Street. After electrification of those lines they were dispersed throughout Britain, excluding the Southern/Western Region (SR/WR), but by the beginning of 1966 just twenty-six remained – none surviving into preservation. I was perhaps fortunate in obtaining runs with ten examples, four being within the NER.

LMS/BR Fairburn Tanks
Designed by C.E. Fairburn, 277 of these 4MT 2-6-4 tanks were constructed between 1945 and 1951 at Brighton and Derby works. Based on his predecessor Stanier's 2-6-4Ts they were allocated throughout Britain (excepting the WR) and used mainly on suburban passenger services. By the beginning of 1966 just ninety remained – two of which (42073/85) have survived into preservation. I was to accrue runs with thirty-one examples, the NER area contributing a healthy twenty-five.

LMS/BR Black 5s
In the history of British steam locomotives, no locomotives have ever been as universally popular as W. Stanier's 5MT 4-6-0 Black 5s. They were undoubtedly the most efficient design of general-purpose mixed-traffic engine ever seen in Britain, subsequently proving suitable for almost any duty. Construction commenced in 1934 and finished in 1951 (suspended 1939–42) eventually totalling 842 being distributed the

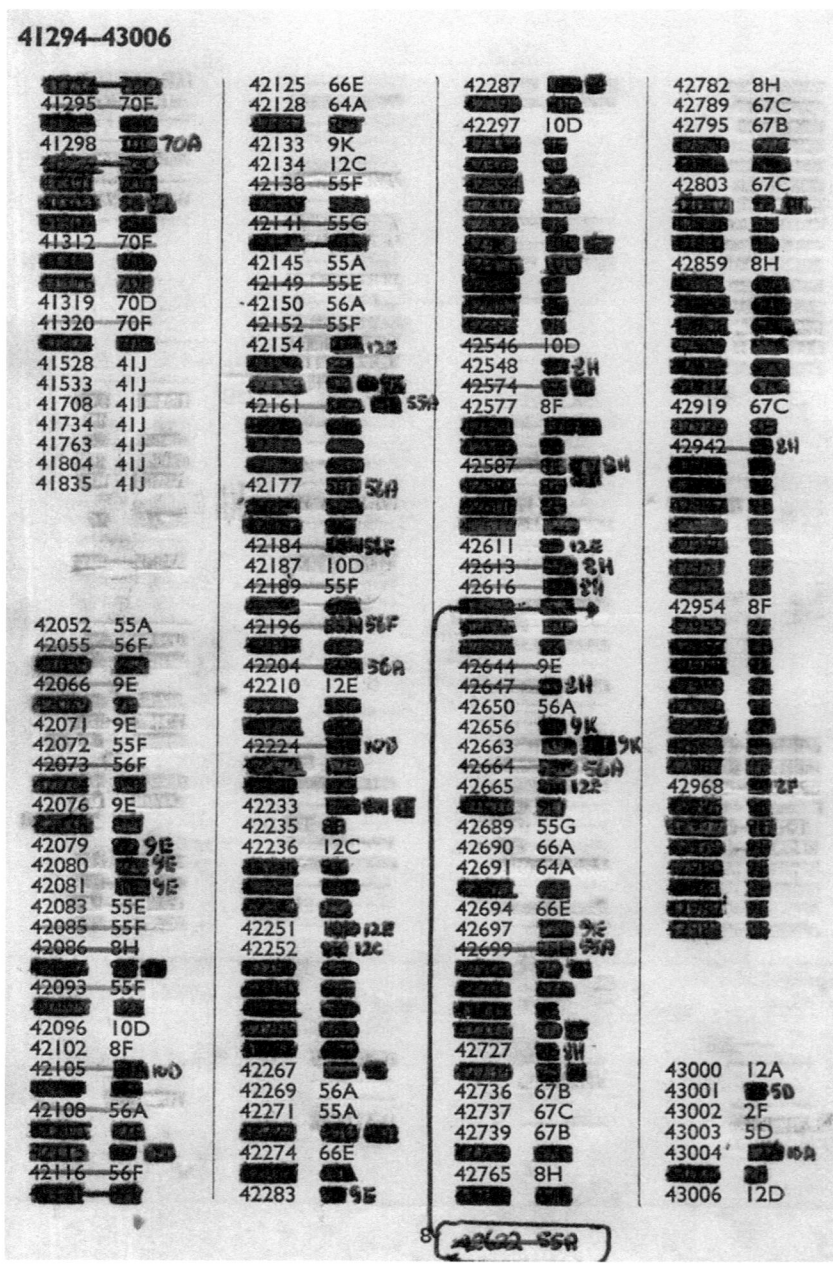

An extract from the Autumn '65 *Locoshed Book* – this page concerning the LMS tanks. These pages required updating every month with information gleaned from either the *LCGB Bulletin* or the Motive Power Miscellany section of *The Railway World* magazine. The blacked-out entries denote that the locomotive has been withdrawn; the right-sided amendment signifies that she has moved sheds and the redlined entry indicates that I have had a run with her.

length and breadth of the former LMS system. Only four examples were named and nationally by the end of 1965 numbers were down to 627 – the NER's quota being a mere three-dozen. Eighteen have survived into preservation. I was to eventually collect runs with exactly a third of the class – my 281st being on Britain's final booked steam passenger train into Liverpool in August 1968. A further eight examples have subsequently been caught in preservation mode.

LMS Jubilees
Constructed between 1934 and 1936 at Crewe, Derby and North British (Glasgow) these Stanier-designed 6P5F 4-6-0 locomotives were widely distributed throughout the former LMS system. In 1935 5552 was named *Silver Jubilee* (celebrating the silver jubilee of King George V), thus giving the marque to the class – all of which referred to either lands in the British Empire, admirals, naval vessels or early locomotives. A total of 189 of these well-proportioned locomotives were built, but a sharp reduction in numbers, commencing during 1962, consequential from a combination of service reductions and dieselisation led them, by my April '66 visit, to have been whittled down to just thirteen.

With the LMR retaining just three (45596 *Bahamas*, 45627 *Sierra Leone* and 45654 *Hood*) it fell to the North Eastern Region's tally of ten to keep the flag flying. That June, however, saw Holbeck's 45660 *Rooke* withdrawn – the remaining nine becoming treated as celebrities. Internally shed staff ensured they were kept in mechanically sound condition while eager young, and not so young, volunteers ensured most, but alas not all, were sent out externally resplendent. Although used throughout the week on parcel and freight services, it was on the summer Saturday passenger services that they came into their own. Courtesy of their Central England base the West Riding Jubilees saw the west coast of Britain at Llandudno and Blackpool, the east at Scarborough and Bridlington, and straddled the Pennines to Carlisle. Four have survived into preservation.

LNER/BR B1s
Introduced in 1942, but constructed over a lengthy ten-year period resulting from wartime conditions, these Thompson-designed 5MT 4-6-0 B1s, eventually totalling 410, were allocated to the Eastern Region (ER) (260), NER (80) and Scottish Region (ScR) (70). Withdrawals, however, began in 1961 accelerated by BR's dieselisation policies on ER and NER passenger services. The first forty constructed were named after various species of antelope thus bestowing their epithet of 'Bongos'. As the numbers increased it became impossible to find enough antelope species to continue this policy, and, apart from some locomotives named after directors of the LNER, most of them remained anonymous. Of the thirty-four remaining on NER metals only eighteen were at the two depots that retained passenger work. Compared with their stablemates (discounting the 6P/5F-rated Jubilees) at Wakefield and Low Moor the B1s, with their superior

The 'amended' B1 pages in my Ian Allan *Combined Volume*.

tractive effort, probably considered themselves better than the work opportunities given them. Mostly coming from sheds within the NER, unlike their sisters having worked Class-1 expresses on the Great Central and East Anglian routes such as *The Master Cutler* and *The Hook Continental*, they had never stretched their legs and in their dotage were eking out their final years on the few lightweight passenger services remaining – fortunately never requiring speeds in excess of 50mph.

Among the survivors were a few 'namers' – a terminology awarded them by over-excited platform enders whenever one hove into view. Even though most were a mere 20-odd years old, young compared with some other pre-nationalisation classes, because of wartime shortages they were, similar to the SR's Q1, cheaply constructed, uncared for and in poor health – appearing to struggle with any 'demanding' work allocated them. Eventually I was to catch runs with a mere sixteen examples of these locomotives; twelve here in the West Riding, three the previous year in Scotland and one of the two preserved, 61264, on a *Steam on the Met* event in 1998.

LNER/BR K1s

Seventy of these North-British-built Peppercorn-designed 6MT 2-6-0s were built over the two years 1949–50 being shared between the ER, NER and ScR. These handsome mixed-traffic locomotives had, because of the modernisation plan, lamentably short lives – the first withdrawal coming in January 1963.

The Main Players

Just one, 62005, made it into preservation. She had become a rail-tour celebrity during her final year (1967) after which she was used as a stationary boiler at the North Tees Refinery at Billingham. Viscount Garnock subsequently purchased her for use as spare parts for his K4 prior to a group of enthusiasts buying and restoring her to working order. She can now be seen at work on the North Yorkshire Moors Railway (NYMR).

So was that it? Not quite, although the aforementioned six classes, all allocated to NER sheds, were the mainstay of expectation; two other LNER types, both having precisely two examples surviving, just about made it into 1966, all four at York. Peppercorn-designed A1 8P Pacifics, 60124 *Kenilworth* and 60145 *Saint Mungo* were sporadically reported on passenger trains during the early months of 1966 but only as a short-notice replacement for diesel failures. *Saint Mungo* herself had marked the official end of express passenger steam on the ECML with an eight-vehicle special between York and Newcastle on 31 December 1965. Advertised as the final run of an A1 Pacific, attaining a maximum of 88mph en route, she was, however, kept as a standby until June 1966. With no examples surviving the cutter's torch, my only haulage with an A1 has been with the newly built and widely travelled 60163 *Tornado*.

Also at 50A were two survivors of another LNER class, Gresley's 6MT 2-6-2 V2s. These locomotives were often lauded as the LNER locomotives that won the war – frequently called upon to haul loads far in excess of their design capabilities. The two remaining examples were also used sporadically to stand in for DL failures, the final member, 60831, being reported working the 08 18 York to Hull, perhaps resulting from a shortage of DMUs, for an entire week during October 1966. Upon 60831's withdrawal that December the York foreman 'borrowed' Holbeck's *Hardy* for several weeks – insisting his firemen were passed out on both two- and three-cylinder locomotives. Fortunately I was to have a run with a V2 in Scotland that August and, in 2010, with the preserved 60800 *Green Arrow*. Then there were the LMS Ivatt 4MT 2-6-0s, affectionately referred to as 'Flying Pigs' (reasons unknown), which had no rostered passenger work but were sometimes turned out by the shed foreman as short-notice replacements for non-availability of the booked power. Patricroft's Standard 5MTs often came over the border with the LMR and we mustn't forget the 'visiting' Britannia's. Carlisle Kingmoor often dispatched its representatives over the Pennines to Yorkshire and, unbeknown to me at the time, until the April of 1966 Stockport-allocated Brits were rostered to and from Leeds on the Aberystwyth/York Travelling Post Office (TPO).

So there we are. With a mere eighty-odd NER-allocated locomotives to catch working approximately thirty often awkward-to-cover passenger services, I perhaps might have concentrated my efforts elsewhere in the country. As a haulage enthusiast you always lived in hope and expectation, and unaware of the paucity on offer I was to return again – and again – determined to hunt down those elusive catches. Please read on and see how I did.

7

DISAPPOINTMENTS GALORE

BUOYED WITH THE success of the previous trip, the second week of May had been selected for my next NER bash – Moors murderers Ian Brady and Myra Hindley being sentenced to life imprisonment dominating newspapers that week. Musically, Manfred Mann once again were topping the charts, this time with *Pretty Flamingo*. The enthusiast fraternity within which I circulated was an eclectic bunch of personalities from all walks of life. The common denominator was the Waterloo rush-hour steam departures where, having ascertained 'what was about', it was often the case that after an initial dispersal, each person having departed after their own particular quest, there was a regrouping later in the evening for a jar or two. Paul, with whom I was to spend the next forty-eight hours, was one of those colleagues, and having also expressed an interest to see steam in another part of Britain, had agreed to accompany me to Yorkshire – I fail to remember which one of us actually planned it! The selected departure date of Thursday 12 May saw us setting forth out of St Pancras on the 21 30 departure. Built in 1868, this Victorian terminus was equipped with a William-Barlow-designed arched train-shed canopy – unique in its day being spaced across 245ft without intermediate support. The station was to survive a closure threat in the 1970s and given a new lease of life, albeit after a vast transformation, as London's Eurostar terminus.

Back in 1966 the overriding fragrance of fumes from the many diesels ticking over was the order of the day and making for what was to become a regular starting point for NER bashes we headed for Sheffield. There we boarded the 02 00 departure for Leeds City – on this occasion with Holbeck's 44854 at the head. Somehow (I was asleep) we lost eighteen minutes en route, which fortuitously reduced the wait at the inhospitable Leeds City station for services to start up to a mere two hours!

Disappointments Galore

The next ten photographs were all taken on Friday 13 May 1966. It's 06 30 in the morning at Bradford Forster Square and 16-year-old Brighton-built Fairburn LMS 2-6-4T 42072 is performing shunting duties. This Manningham (Bradford) allocated 4MT was, upon the closure of 55F, transferred across the city to Bradford's other shed, Low Moor, being withdrawn in the NER cull of October 1967.

Steam-powered named trains were becoming scarce as the years went by. It's now 07 30 at Leeds City station and *The Cornishman* has been brought the 13½ miles from Bradford by Holbeck (Leeds) allocated Fairburn 42161. Starting out of Bradford at 07 02 the train would now be worked forward by a Brush Type 4 diesel the 410 miles to Penzance where it was due to arrive at 17 35. This 1948 Derby-built tank was to be withdrawn that December.

Over to Bradford with another recently delivered 'Splutterbug' a second 55A locomotive, in the form of Fairburn tank 42161, was already heating the 07 02 *The Cornishman* departure. Steam-worked named trains were becoming as rare as hen's teeth and this was recorded (in capital letters) in my notebook with much flourish!

Ominously it was now several hours into Friday the 13th as we embarked on what turned out to be an abortive attempt at tracking steam-operated services by travelling over, courtesy of a four-month-old Brush Type 4 D1984 working the 08 35 *North Briton* departure, to the confluence city of the three Ridings, York. The present-day York station was first opened by the NER in 1877 and, at the time, was the largest station in the world – being provided with thirteen platforms. It had replaced the somewhat inconveniently sited predecessor, which, by being built as a terminus within the city walls, required all trains calling there to reverse. The fine overall roof still stands today overlooked by the Scarborough bricked Royal Station Hotel, opened but a year later. Expanded to sixteen platforms in 1909, it was heavily bombed during the Second World War. Remodelling in 1988 led to several bay platforms succumbing to an inevitable extra car park. We were there for the 10 08 departure for Poole – shown in Roger's book as steam worked. It wasn't, but a compensatory unauthorised bunk around the shed, camera in hand, was undertaken – the results still nostalgically often browsed through to this day.

York once boasted two steam sheds: York South, which housed LMS locomotives and York North, which housed the LNER locomotives. The South shed closed in 1961, boosting the North's allocation to over 185. Previously consisting of four roundhouses in 1954 two were demolished and replaced by a straight shed 50A, although closing to steam in June 1967, continued to operate as a diesel depot for a further fifteen years. The site is now part of the National Railway Museum, which, in 2015, celebrates its 40th birthday.

On that fine May morning we were able to wander at will (unchallenged) among these workhorses at rest. The intoxicating aroma of coal, steam, smoke and oil of these hallowed edifices, although similar scenes are created on a smaller scale at many preserved railways, can never, on a size such as here, be replicated. It was as if we had walked through a TARDIS (*Doctor Who* was a popular TV show of the period) and gone from a fresh-smelling, open-air world into a strange sepulchral atmosphere, silent but for the hiss of escaping steam. Although this was my only NER shed bunked, when visiting other sheds, such as Bournemouth, Shrewsbury, Carlisle and several Glaswegian locations, if challenged by 'authority' after producing our BR identity cards we were usually allowed to continue with the comment 'I haven't seen you', in case we were to befall any mishap. The thirty locomotives present are detailed here:

YORK SHED (50A) – Friday 13th MAY 1966 – 1100

Status	Class	Number	Total
In steam	LMS 4MT LNER V2 LNER B1 LNER K1 WD Aus BR 9F	43071, 43133, 43138 60806 61319 62028, 62042 90078 92006, 92008, 92239	11
Dead	LMS 4MT LNER A1 LNER V2 LNER B1 LNER K1 LNER J27 WD Aus BR 9F	43123 60145 *Saint Mungo* 60831 61017 *Bushbuck*, 61035 *Pronghorn*, 61218 62012, 62046, 62065 65894 90254, 90347, 90395, 90517 92231	15
Stored	LMS 4MT LNER V2 LNER B1 WD Aus	43126 60886 61218 90518	4

We now move to York where later that morning Peppercorn-designed 2-6-0 K1 62028 was on empty coaching stock (ECS) duties. All seventy members of this class were built at North British – this 1949 example being withdrawn that November.

With planned steam haulages not materialising a compensatory bash of York MPD was undertaken. The end looks near for York's 17-year-old K1 62012 with her chimney being covered with sacking. Despite appearances she was to survive a further year, ending her days at Sunderland in May 1967.

Looking somewhat forlorn, 43-year-old Darlington built J27 65894 was to become one of the final five being withdrawn at Sunderland in September 1967. However fortune shone upon her and having undergone a 10-year overhaul she has returned, in 2016, to operational status at the North Yorkshire Moors Railway.

The only Peppercorn-designed LNER 4-6-2 A1 I witnessed in service was 60145 *Saint Mungo*. This Darlington-built 17-year-old 8P had sporadically rescued a few trains on the ECML due to diesel failures and in December 1965 had powered a special 'end of class' outing to Newcastle and back. Although she was in a line of dead locomotives the official withdrawal date was documented as being the following month. I had to wait thirty-four years before I obtained a run with an A1, courtesy of the 2008-constructed 60163 *Tornado*.

Between 1943 and 1946 a total of 733 of these Riddles-designed War Department 2-8-0s, nicknamed 'Dub-dees', were built for use both here and in northern Europe to 'get things going' after the devastation of the war. Here 22-year-old North British-built 90395 appears to be receiving works attention at her home shed. She was subsequently transferred to Sunderland, being withdrawn there six months later.

A total of 162 of these Ivatt-designed LMS 4MT 2-6-0 locomotives were built – 43071 being at Darlington in 1950. She was transferred to Blyth and was withdrawn from there in March 1967.

There was nothing quite like a steam shed for atmosphere. Horwich-built 'Flying Pig' 43123 is seen surrounded by all the detritus of a working shed. This site is now occupied by the National Railway Museum.

Disappointments Galore

Another wonderful vista from a bygone age as four home shed allocated locomotives from four different classes surround the turntable. From left to right we have: 92006, a 1954 Crewe-built Riddles-designed 2-10-0 (a total of 251 being constructed between 1954 and 1960) which ended her days at Wakefield eleven months later; then WD 90078 and B1 61017 *Bushbuck* – both not seeing the year out – and finally fresh from station pilot duties K1 62028.

The front cover of an EP given to me one Christmas.

Although the majority of V2s remaining in Britain were NER based the only one I caught a run with was Dundee's 60813 – seen here after arrival at Edinburgh Waverley on 13 August 1966 with the 09 10 Summer Saturday Dundee Tay Bridge to Blackpool North. Having targeted alleged V2-operated services during both summers of '65 and '66, I was indeed fortunate to finally catch a run with one. This 29-year-old Darlington-built locomotive was withdrawn that September.

With both of us being railwaymen you would have thought that we could have read timetables with an element of accuracy. However, resulting from a foul-up of some sort, having travelled via Leeds to Wakefield, we became stranded for an hour at Wakefield's Kirkgate station. This station was opened by the Manchester and Leeds Railway Company in 1840 and until 1867, upon the opening of Wakefield's other station at Westgate, was the only one for the city. Always the poorer relation from then on, the station had by the time of our visit an air of neglect about it – not helped by many panes missing from the 'nearly' overall roof. It was to be completely removed six years later, presumably resulting from its perilous condition. Often in the news in respect of vandalism and other antisocial activities, a royal visit by Prince Charles (who rededicated Britannia 70013 *Oliver Cromwell* there) during 2012 kickstarted a multimillion-pound improvement scheme. Once again, making the most of the situation, out came the camera to capture the parade of Austerity WD 2-8-0s passing through or stopping for water/crew change working a seemingly endless procession of lengthy freight services.

Returning to that Friday, 13 May 1966, resulting from an error in timetable reading we became 'stranded' at Wakefield for several hours, so out came the camera to capture the scenes, the next eight pictures all being taken on that day. At Wakefield Kirkgate we see WD 2-8-0 90099 waiting signals for the road to Wakefield shed (56A). She was withdrawn when her home shed of Goole closed in June 1967.

A seemingly continuous stream of steam-hauled freight trains passed through Wakefield Kirkgate during the hour we were there that day. Here North-British-built 8F 90407 heads westwards with a lengthy load. Withdrawal came from her home shed of Wakefield a year later.

Regaining the footplate having contacted the signalman, presumably asking for the road to the shed, Wakefield's WD 90642 awaits the signal. This 1944 Vulcan Foundry (Newton-le-Willows) built locomotive was to be transferred to Normanton, being withdrawn from there in September 1967.

An artefact from a bygone age: instructions for 'visiting' engine men from 'foreign' depots at the dilapidated Wakefield Kirkgate station.

One of Normanton's two Fairburn tanks, 1951 Brighton-built 42083 wanders into Wakefield Kirkgate with a lightweight van service. Even though she lasted until the October 1967 cull I never caught up with her!

Holbeck-allocated 4MT 43130 struggles to start a heavy ECS up the incline out of Leeds Central. This Horwich-built 15-year-old locomotive was withdrawn in July 1967. A point of interest not realised until researching for this book is the wagon hoist in the background – all that remains today of the site.

Waiting her next turn of duty at Leeds City is Derby-built 18-year-old Fairburn 4MT 42196. Then allocated to Neville Hill, she was transferred to Low Moor (thus allowing me to catch her on a Bradford Exchange portion) upon 55H's closure to steam the following month.

Returning to Leeds for the 16 10 Cleethorpes departure only to find it formed of a two-car 'bog cart' (a despised all-too-common hybrid – neither locomotive nor coaches and officially classified as a DMU) rather than the expected B1 (*Railway World* magazine subsequently reported the train as having been dieselised four weeks previously!) we, at last after nine steamless hours, finally achieved success on the 16 45 Leeds Central to Doncaster – Holbeck's 44852 working this train that day. Little did we realise at the time that this working was the last steam-operated passenger service into the Eastern Region – Doncaster (36A) being the final ER steam shed and closing the following month.

Roger's book of steam passenger workings, although having unintentionally misled us throughout the day, was now proving instrumental to our movements. By boarding the rear coaches of the 16 20 Kings Cross to Leeds Central at Doncaster, upon arrival at Wakefield Westgate the Bradford Exchange portion was detached and worked forward the 17 miles by Holyhead allocated Black 5 44770. This was my first trip on one of the Bradford portions – a note in my book testifying 'the line was chock-a-block with steam'. I was soon to realise that these trains were to become an essential ingredient to sate a haulage devotee's appetite for new catches on many further visits to the area.

As it was my first visit into Bradford Exchange station, a location that perhaps because of its varied steam powered services became a firm favourite of mine, a further brief history lesson is due. This was the second station in Bradford, being opened four years later (1850) than its Midland Railway counterpart as a joint enterprise between the Lancashire and Yorkshire and Great Northern Railways. In 1867 the Leeds, Bradford & Halifax Joint Railway, which had previously used the nearby Adolphus Street terminus, joined the melee by building a connecting link. Proving inadequate for purpose, in 1880 it was completely rebuilt – the ten-platformed terminus being christened Exchange after the nearby wool exchange – and was equipped with two arched roofs and classical Corinthian columns down the centre, next to which the Great Victoria hotel was erected. Jubilees, B1s, LMS tanks, LMS Moguls, Black 5s – they could all be counted upon to put in an appearance on a summer Saturday. To me, being a relatively small terminus, it epitomised the steam era, with locomotives often standing at buffer stops for lengthy periods and with their steam and smoke entrapped under the sooty, grimy train shed roof the station just simply oozed atmosphere. If only I could have canned some!

Contributing to the scenario immediately outside the station was a 1-in-50 incline. This meant locomotives having to work hard straightaway upon departure, indeed the lengthy summer Saturday services bound for the East and West coastal resorts required banking locomotives to Bowling Junction, and, as a result of the original tunnel being cut away to provide room for the doubling of tracks, the high walls either side amplified their exertions wonderfully.

A late evening shot of Low Moor's B1 61014 *Oribi* being prepared in the locomotive sidings at Bradford Exchange to work the 21 25 portion for Wakefield Westgate (en route to Kings Cross). Naively walking over to Forster Square for a tank trip into Leeds, I missed the opportunity to travel with her – she being transferred away to Blyth that August from where this 1946 Darlington-built locomotive was withdrawn four months later.

In 1973, traffic having fallen away, the station was rebuilt 50 yards south and on the site of the closed Bridge Street goods depot – subsequently being renamed Bradford Interchange in 1983 as a more representative description of its purpose as a transport hub. From the 1970s, for many years, BR considered there was insufficient demand warranting through services to London – a situation benefitting from privatisation with the Grand Central train operating company rectifying the situation in 2010. Back to 1966 and naively ignoring B1 61014 *Oribi* (an opportunity lost – she was transferred away to Blyth that August and withdrawn four months later) being prepared to work the 21 25 portion for Wakefield, we took the short walk (although the current relocated stations are further apart, a proposed tram/train link connecting both with Leeds/Bradford airport is being actively considered) over to Forster Square and headed back to Leeds with, by changing en route at Shipley, runs with two further examples of Fairburn tanks. This was becoming an increasingly successful junket – or so we convinced ourselves!

Many changes, to the detriment of steam chasers, had taken place when the summer timetable had commenced on 18 April that year. The Leeds/Morecambe services had gone DMU, the last Harrogate to diesel locomotive (DL) and, more relevant to where we were that night, the Aberystwyth/York TPO, previously worked by a stud of LMR-allocated Brits west of Leeds had also gone DL. Why relevant? For overnight accommodation that night we had calculatingly travelled west to the then incumbent prime minister's (Harold Wilson) birthplace of Huddersfield to board the eastbound TPO, thus giving us at least two hours on board a warm comfortable train. Before departing Leeds we noted Jubilee 45647 *Sturdee* simmering tantalisingly facing north – perhaps to work our train forward to York? Not so – English Electric Type 4 'Long Pong' D353 worked through. The self-explanatory nickname to these DLs was one given by steam followers, the more common perhaps being 'Whistler' – a reference to the noise emanating from the sound of their turbocharger. A total of 400 of these machines had been built and, having displaced steam over the WCML, were now, resulting from electrification south of Crewe, themselves homeless and were to be found anywhere throughout the LMR and ER/NER regions.

With the option of a long cold wait at Leeds before the daytime services commenced, there was no alternative other than staying aboard to York. What luck we did as *Sturdee* must have worked to York on a preceding parcels/van train and had been turned to work back to Leeds on the 04 35 departure – with us aboard! I had never heard of Farnley Junction, where she was allocated and hadn't a clue as to its location, but, with only a mere dozen Jubilees remaining in the country, I cared not – an appreciative redlined entry in my book was enough! After sleepless nights, trying to second-guess moves, missed connections, abortive journeys – a catch such as this made it all worthwhile. The light was just about good enough upon arriving into Leeds at 05 15 for a (poor quality) shot of her – just to prove indisputably that not only did I travel with *Sturdee* but as a confirmatory piece of evidence of the insanity of our chosen hobby.

The following five photographs were all taken during our activities on the next day, Saturday 14 May 1966. Ever the nocturnal traveller, it's 05 15 in the morning and LMS Stanier-designed 6P5F Jubilee 45647 *Sturdee* rests from her labours having arrived into Leeds City with the 04 35 from York. A total of 189 of these 4-6-0s were built, *Sturdee* herself at Crewe in 1935. Allocated to Farnley Junction, she was transferred to Holbeck upon its closure that November – being withdrawn in April 1967.

After that pleasing catch our luck returned to normal and, having trekked over to Hull for what Roger had shown in his book as B1 operated service, the 08 55 Hull to Doncaster was added to the list of steam casualties! With no alternative we travelled on it (D1516) and returned to Wakefield once again for what we knew was guaranteed steam on the Bradford portions. Or was it? Nothing could be taken for granted during those dying days of steam. Displaced DLs from elsewhere could have been sent to the area. Fortune, however, favours the brave and gratifyingly the portions turned up trumps with two LNER B1s (neither seeing the year out) and a Fairburn tank being caught over a period of six hours. That might not seem many for such a lengthy period of time but during a two-hour wait at Wakefield in the mid afternoon, never missing an excuse for an extra steam run, we squeezed in an 11-mile trip down the line to the 100-year-old ex-West Riding and Grimsby Joint Line station of South Elmsall – on a service we knew was steam-operated, having caught it the previous day – with Holbeck's 44853 on the Doncaster train. This completed a run of three consecutively numbered Black 5s 44852/3/4 – gloatingly redlined upon returning home! And so ended a run of twelve required locomotives.

Fairburn 42142, built at Derby in 1950, departs Wakefield Westgate at 12 15 with the Bradford Exchange portion of the 09 25 Kings Cross to Leeds Central. We had not travelled with her for two reasons: 1) she was booked to return from Bradford at 15 05 (which we hoped to catch); and 2) a far superior requirement had been seen arriving from Wakefield shed (B1 61386) in readiness for the next portion departure at 13 41. Initially allocated to St Albans, she was to spend twelve years in Scotland before being withdrawn from her home shed of Low Moor just five weeks later.

North British 1943-built WD 90200 storms up the gradient into Wakefield Westgate on a freight they were most at home on – coal. This Wakefield-allocated 2-8-0 was transferred to Sunderland from where she was withdrawn in July 1967.

The aforementioned Low-Moor-allocated B1 4-6-0 61386 at Bradford Exchange having worked the 17 miles from Wakefield Westgate with the three-coach portion off the 10 20 from Kings Cross. These portions were a godsend in respect of catching runs with this LNER class of steam locomotives, and the sporadic successes in catching them made the long trek north worthwhile. She was transferred to Blyth three months later from where she was withdrawn in December 1966.

Vulcan Foundry 1947-built B1 61161 at Bradford Exchange with the 21 25 portion for Wakefield Westgate. Having noted the previous day this train was B1-operated, we changed our plans to catch her on the inwards working – the 18 25 portion ex-Wakefield. She, like the majority of B1s in the West Riding, was withdrawn in December that year.

A perfect example depicting the dirt ridden grimy scenario associated with the steam age. An undated shot of the lineup of a Black 5 and two Fairburn tanks at Bradford Exchange. (Alan (Nobby) Hayes)

Extract from notebook.

The football specials from London had yet to arrive back in Yorkshire that FA Cup day – Everton having beaten Sheffield Wednesday 3-2 at Wembley. However, all still peaceful at Bradford Exchange and having somewhat surprisingly witnessed Jubilee 45694 *Bellerophon* arriving in there on a Wakefield portion earlier that evening we somehow ascertained that she was booked back out on the 22 00 Huddersfield one-coach departure – overpowered or what!

After forty-eight hours together, Paul and I parted company. Although we both wanted a run with her, Paul decided it was worth the lengthy wait – the result of which meant heading home from Manchester over the WCML into Euston. Taking into consideration that the closure of the ex-GC line into Marylebone had been announced, I opted for an earlier return journey south on the 22 50 Manchester Central/Marylebone train. The attraction of collecting two further runs with steam, i.e. Manchester to Guide Bridge and Leicester Central to Woodford Halse, was, in my opinion, of greater persuasion. This was an occasion where we steam followers sometimes differed in our needs – I am unable to put into print what Paul said when, the following month, we caught *Bellerophon* out of Blackpool! As an aside for the football aficionados among the readers that year Liverpool were the 1st division champions, Manchester City the 2nd, Hull City the 3rd and Doncaster Rovers the 4th.

8

THE ALNWICK ADVENTURE

WHILE THE MAINSTAY of this book is about my journeys in Yorkshire, with readers' permission I'd like to enact the writers' license and relate one of my forays elsewhere within the North Eastern Region of British Railways. Although, in Chapter 5, I detailed the fact that Tweedmouth (more pertinently the sub shed at Alnmouth) provided K1 Moguls for the Alnwick branch, in the spring of 1966 I was unaware of that fact. Persistent rumours were circulating amongst us haulage bashers that the Alnwick branch shuttles (as compared with the through-DMU services from Newcastle) were steam operated and were the preserve of the 1949-built Peppercorn-designed K1 Moguls to boot. The branch was a long way from any other steam passenger-operated areas in the North East and with no other friends/colleagues having visited to confirm it we, Alan (another SR devotee) and I, made the decision to investigate. We were the guinea pigs – we could be wasting our valuable time. Such was the search-and-find scenario we encountered back then.

With hope in our hearts, and Frank Sinatra's *Strangers in the Night* topping the charts, we set forth out of Kings Cross on Friday 17 June 1966, a week after the sitcom *Till Death Us Do Part* commenced regular broadcasting, on the 23 45 Kings Cross to Newcastle. This train, readers may recall, was the same one I had travelled on nearly two years previously when venturing north for the very first time. Back then Newcastle was awash with LNER steam, but by June 1966 it was the centre of a diesel-infested area. It wasn't looking at all promising and after a two-hour connectional wait we headed the 34¾ miles north with Type 4 D353 to the branch junction station of Alnmouth. Nothing ventured, nothing gained, but boy did this one pay off! Waiting in the adjacent bay platform was Tweedmouth's K1 62011 with the 07 50 departure for Alnwick. This 3-mile-long branch, opened in 1850, was continued through to Coldstream, a junction station on the Tweedmouth/St Boswell line, in 1887. To avoid the wrath of the land-owning Duke of Northumberland, whose Alnwick Castle has been subsequently used as Hogwarts School in the Harry Potter films, a somewhat expensive diversion requiring a tunnel and viaduct at Edlingham was constructed – the relocation of Alnwick station nearer the town centre being undertaken at the same time. Passenger traffic over the sparsely populated and somewhat circuitous section beyond Alnwick, however, was unable to compete with local bus services and the line closed to passengers in 1930. Retained for freight the line was breached midway at Iderton by a storm in 1948 – the remaining stub south to Alnwick closing completely five years later.

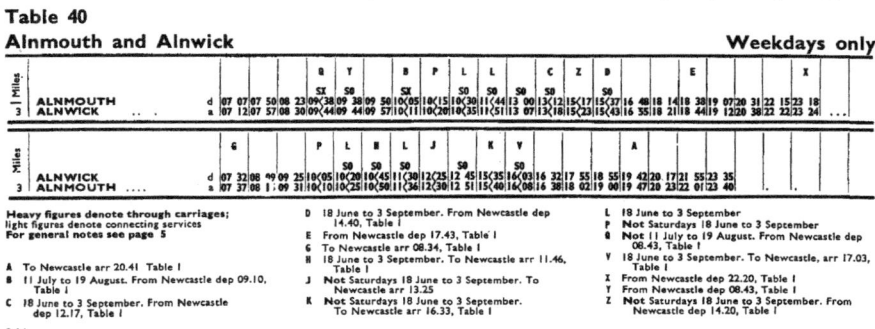

The Alnwick branch timetable. All the through workings to/from Newcastle were DMU operated. The remainder, until our day of travel of Saturday 18 June 1966, were steam operated.

Alan and I had made the long trek north to the 3-mile branch off of the ECML at Alnmouth on a wing and a prayer – persistent rumours circulating amongst the enthusiast fraternity conjecturing that the branch trains were steam operated. Unaware that Tweedmouth shed, where the branch locomotives were allocated, was closing to steam the following Monday, we were fortunate in catching steam on the branch at all. With my head hanging out of the window this shot shows 1949-built K1 2-6-0 62011 (cleaned by the MNA) bringing the 07 50 ex-Alnmouth into the somewhat dilapidated terminal station of Alnwick. (Alan (Nobby) Hayes)

BR-built mogul 62011 prepares to return to Alnmouth with the 08 09 departure – she was one of the final four representatives to be withdrawn from Tyne Dock in September 1967. Later that day, as a finale before the branch line's dieselisation, 9F 92099 was turned out, but even had we known that it would have been a long wait! The branch itself succumbed to complete closure in January 1968.

The somewhat overgenerous 'new' Alnwick station, by now in a somewhat neglected condition, provided a wonderful backdrop to photographs taken on the day of our visit when the K1 was running round her two-coach train.

With only the one steam locomotive in circulation and, having successfully completed our mission, just over half an hour later found us returning south from Alnmouth on a bone-shaking Metro-Cammell bog cart en route to the then steam Mecca of the West Riding. We were, at the time, completely unaware of the fact that 18 June was the last day of steam-operated services on the branch – 9F 92099 being turned out for the afternoon/evening shuttles. Earlier that year, reports in *The Railway World* revealed, V2 60836 en route home from York to Dundee was 'borrowed' by Alnmouth shed to help out during a shortage of power for the shed's diagrammed coal trains. Not being suitable over certain routes she was put to work on the Alnwick services.

Tweedmouth and the sub shed at Alnmouth closed to steam on that day. Three months prior to our visit a notice of the branch's closure had been posted with that very weekend being its final day. Strong local opposition, although initially thwarting BR's plans, was eventually disregarded and services ceased in January 1968. Although quoting heavy financial losses was it more than just coincidence that an expensive bridge would have had to have been constructed for the line to be carried over the proposed Alnwick bypass? The somewhat ostentatious station, however, remains to this day albeit in use as a retail outlet containing, amongst other shops, one of Britain's largest second-hand bookshops. A group of volunteers calling themselves the Aln Valley Railway Society has (at the time of writing, 2015) commenced running passenger trains over a short section of the original trackbed midway along the branch.

Arriving back into Leeds just before midday we came across Manningham Fairburn 42189 working the 10 39 ex-Sheffield forward to Bradford Forster Square only minutes later. A stroll across to Exchange found Mirfield's Black 5 45208 ready to depart for Wakefield with the 13 05 portion. Although she still had a 56D shed plate on her boiler, I suspect Low Moor (to where she was officially transferred within weeks) had already purloined her. She was in such fine form that, by arriving into Wakefield Westgate six minutes early, we were able to dash through the subway just making an (on paper) minus two-minute connection into a returning Bradford portion. Why the hurry? A rare appearance of an Ivatt 4MT 'Flying Pig' on a passenger train – Wakefield's 43070 being turned out for the 14 16 arrival into the Exchange that day!

Oh what a joy these portions were – back-to-back runs with two named (my first!) B1s was to follow; 61240 *Harry Hinchcliffe* and 61022 *Sassaby*, neither of which saw the year out. Taking into consideration their comparative rareness throughout the country I think I appreciated catching runs with the few remaining LNER B1s more than anything else. Our good fortune, however, was to suffer a temporary blip at that point with nearly an hour spent at Shipley waiting for a portion ex-Leeds City – disappointingly producing D1767 on a train normally steam operated! Anyway, having decided to return south once again via the ex-GC routed 22 50 Manchester

Mirfield (a depot with no passenger work) allocated Black 5 45208 at Bradford Exchange on 18 June 1966 with the 13 05 portion for Wakefield Westgate. A bountiful 842 of these LMS 4-6-0 5MT 'maids of all work' were built – 45208 at Armstrong-Whitworth in 1935. She was transferred to Low Moor from where she was withdrawn upon that shed's closure in October 1967.

Having made a tight cross-platform connection at Wakefield off the previous train, once more we shuttled back to Wakefield Westgate where, after arrival with the 15 05 portion ex-Bradford Exchange, we see B1 61240 *Harry Hinchcliffe*. She is about to be detached – a second locomotive pulling the portion back into the sidings before then propelling it onto the Leeds Central to Kings Cross train. Always grateful for a 'namer' this 1947-built locomotive was to be withdrawn from Wakefield just six months later.

Central/Marylebone, there was just time to catch one further Fairburn, Wakefield's 42196 being caught out to Halifax on the 19 10 departure. This was a Bradford Exchange portion detached at Wakefield Westgate off the 15 25 Kings Cross/Leeds Central, which reversed at Bradford Exchange for an 8-mile extension to Halifax. These somewhat unusual once-a-day workings were nectar to the steam follower as 99 per cent of them would be steam worked. It wasn't the greatest steam-mileage weekend but with a K1, a Flying Pig and two 'namers' I wasn't going to complain.

17-18-19/6/66   42073 - 1520
                 61382   6/7
                           90
                         3/5   29

2122	14h	SMY	5310	1845	Ship 1 2L	D1767	
2057	10L	EK	—	1852	Brad FS 1L	—	
2345	4L	KX	D1528	1910	Brad Ex 1E	42196	
0505	5E	NEW	—	1924	Halifax ✓	—	
0700	1	NEW	D353 (check mileage)	1994	Halifax 2L	NR	
0748	1L	ALN	—	2037	Man Ex	—	
0750	2L	ALN	62011	2250	Man Lim	45239	
0757	2L	ALN	—	⎧	Guide B/	27001	
0809	5L	ALN	62011	⎨	Sheff Vic	D1547	
0816	5L	ALN	—	⎨	Lerce Cen	49941	
0818	8L	ALN	NOT RECORDED	⎩ ↓	Wood H	D5077	
0912	1L	NEW	—	0519	Mans 7E	—	
0935		NEW	D168	0608	VA	1L	5631
1056		YTAY	—	0616	HRN	..	⎫
1112	1L	YORK	NOT RECORDED	06	HRN	2L	5255
1149	5L	Leeds City	—	0647	BN	2L	—
1206	2L	Leeds City	42189				
1233	2F	Brad FS	—				
1305	✓	Brad Ex	45208				
1339	6E	Low W	—				
1341	5L	Wake W	43070				
1416	4L	Brad E	—		268.50		
1505	—	Brad Ex	61240 *		128.00		
1542	2E	Wake W.	—		80.50		
1655	✓	Wake	61022 *				
1732	2L	Brad Ex	—				
1743		Brad FS	NR				
1748		Ship	—				

Extract from notebook.

9

WHERE ARE THOSE ELUSIVE JUBILEES?

BY THE SUMMER of 1966, with the Beatles topping the charts with their tenth hit – *Paperback Writer* – a mere nine NER-allocated Jubilees remained. Having already obtained runs with *Kolhapur* and *Sturdee* I began deliberately blitzing train services they were likely to be working in a bid to catch runs with the other seven. If I didn't know where any particular locomotive was then an exchange of information at about 8 a.m. on a Saturday morning with 'platform enders' at either Bradford Exchange or Leeds City soon rectified the shortfall in knowledge for that day. Having ascertained, if known, which Jubilee was working what train, plans for the day's activities were made. If you had missed or were unable to catch the outward working then, failures permitting, you could home in on the return later that day. And so, on that last Saturday of June, Paul and I, having travelled down on the Barrow 'kippers' and had several runs with Black/Standard 5s and Brits over the WCML, found ourselves at Blackpool's North station.

Blackpool rose to prominence as a major centre of tourism with the arrival of the railways during the 1840s. The railways made it much easier and cheaper for visitors from the industrialised regions of Northern England to reach Blackpool, which by 1881 had a population of 14,000 complete with all the trappings expected of a seaside resort, e.g. promenade, sandy beaches, piers, fortune-tellers, public houses, trams, donkey rides, fish-and-chip shops, the tower, illuminations and theatres. By 1901 the population of Blackpool was 47,000, and its place as 'the archetypal British seaside resort' was secured. By the 1960s, however, the attraction of the sunnier climes of Spain and Italy had supplanted Blackpool's status as a leading resort and Britons, using their increasing prosperity, began holidaying abroad. Nevertheless Blackpool's urban fabric and economy remains relatively undiversified and continues to attract millions of visitors every year – albeit, these days, mostly by road.

As an aside, not long after the end of steam in 1968 I made a spur-of-the-moment decision to attend a performance by one of the top pop stars of the time, Cilla Black. Not having booked a seat I had to stand at the back – after which, due to the absence of returning overnight trains, I went in search of a B&B. Having developed a post-steam crush for her – she having been portrayed as single to promote record sales amongst males – I was devastated upon learning of her betrothal to her manager months later! I have returned to Blackpool, taking my wife and daughter to see the illuminations, on a couple of occasions since – deliberately selecting the comfort of the long-disappeared loco-hauled services.

Anyway, I digress. Back to 1966 and there were still a fair number of holiday extras run by BR, all dealt with, resulting from the money-orientated sale of Blackpool Central's prime site, at Blackpool's North station. Having espied Wakefield's 45694 *Bellerophon* at the head of the 13 25 departure for Yorkshire when arriving a mere eighteen minutes prior we were late onto the train itself, unexpectedly having to obtain regulation tickets from the booking office. This was somewhat farcical as other than us there were only three people in the first two coaches! This eight-coach train was booked 1¾ hours non-stop to the Calder Valley station of Hebden Bridge. After passing through Poulton-le-Fylde, where passengers could then change trains for Fleetwood, the next notable junction (to Blackpool's other station – the South née Central) was Kirkham & Wesham. This location was to become much frequented over the following eighteen months because conveniently situated next to it was a

Blackpool Central – closed later that year because the ground became too valuable to keep under Beeching's 'must make the railways pay their way' axe. On 22 August 1964 Carlisle Upperby's Patriot 45527 *Southport* and Newton Heath's Black 5 45339 prepare to depart with returning holiday extras. I was more intent on line coverage that day and failed to appreciate the rareness of a ride with one of the few remaining Patriots – she was withdrawn that December.

Blackpool North, the station that dealt with all the holiday services after the Central's demise, sees Wakefield's Jubilee 45694 *Bellerophon* awaiting departure on 25 June 1966 with the 13 25 for Bradford Exchange/Leeds Central. It was the second occasion this Summer Saturday train ran that year and was the commencement of my attempt in hunting down all the remaining nine required Jubilees allocated within the North Eastern Region.

public house where most summer Saturdays in 1966/7, after a hard day's chasing on WCML metals, all us haulage fanatics congregated.

We had come out of Preston on a portion off of a London train and had one-and-a-quarter hours to neck as much frothy northern beer as we could while comparing catches and sightings prior to a Liverpool-bound service calling to collect us over imbibed gricers. Continuing with our Jubilee journey, having taken water at Lea Road troughs, most of which I am sure ended up over the first coach, we then passed through the station of Preston, which in just over two years' time was to witness steam's final booked passenger train. Preston was centrally positioned for a steam basher and many many hours were spent waiting for whatever was running to appear – very few trains failing to call there. Always on the lookout for mates wherever we travelled it was of necessity to lean out of the window and if espying some friends point to the front and shout 'see what we're behind' (or words to that effect) as loud as possible!

Now taking the Blackburn route eastwards, we passed the hallowed ground of Lostock Hall MPD. This shed was destined to become one of the last three in Britain at which steam was to be located and (if the publisher allows me a follow-up book) can be dealt with in a north-western companion to this. Onwards we went and after Blackburn and Burnley, and having battled the 1-in-68 incline to the 749ft-high Copy Pit summit on the Lancashire/Yorkshire border, breasted at 19mph, we then attained the max of the journey – 54½mph between the Calder Valley station stops of Hebden and Sowerby bridges. Bradford, we decided to travel in the three - coach Leeds portion – being detached at Halifax. Fairburn tank 42108 was duly waiting, coupled up and then a twenty-minute delay ensued while a tail lamp was found! This delay meant that instead of travelling back to Bradford out of Leeds Central on a steam service we had to suffer a DMU. Even this train was late and arrived into the Exchange station at 17 10 vice 17 05, resulting in a tight cross-platform connection to catch Fairburn 42055, which was on the 17 10 portion to Wakefield. The Low Moor driver, however, kindly waited for us (the guard had already given the right away) after shouts from us to 'hold on a minute mate' from our DMU which, luckily for us, arrived in the adjacent platform.

The working arrangement for the southbound portions at Wakefield Westgate, in order for attachment to the main Leeds Central/Kings Cross train, was as follows. After the Bradford portion had come to a stand a second locomotive would draw it back into a siding, await the arrival of the Leeds service, and propel it onto the rear. On this day Ivatt Mogul 43137 performed that shunt so, never sure when any steam movement, whether shunt or long distance, might be the only chance of haulage with that particular locomotive, we jumped back aboard and claimed a run with her – only to find she then proceeded to work the next detachment for Bradford off a Kings Cross/Leeds service on which we planned to travel on anyway!

Another Fairburn tank, Low Moor's 42177, was waiting at Bradford to take the train on to Halifax but was eventually cancelled due to the non-appearance of a guard – I never did obtain a run with her! That was enough of the NER that day and, with a running total of nine new haulages (and most importantly one of the required Jubilees), we headed off to Manchester for what became my final homeward-bound journey over the ex-GC.

The following Friday a valuable day's leave was taken. Why? Well the 13 27 Fridays and Saturdays only (FSO) train from Manchester Victoria to Edinburgh Waverley had commenced running and it was a steam chaser's delight. A total of six locomotives, if you include the bankers up Shap and Beattock, were caught on this 222-mile journey. Although the main thrust of the weekend was the NER Jubilees, we were always on the lookout for unusual short-dated workings, the likelihood of them being steam worked being a high probability. We (Bob and I), having arrived into Edinburgh over an hour late at 19 40, travelled north to Kirkcaldy to board the 19 45 Friday Only (FO) Aberdeen to York. This train ran for just three Fridays and, unaware that it was a one that required regulation tickets, we nearly weren't allowed to board until producing the ever-reliable passport to most problems – our BR identity cards! Ferryhill (Aberdeen) fortuitously turned out one of their Black 5s and, after she handed the train over to the inevitable Brush 4 at Edinburgh, we settled down (stretched out in a compartment) for several hours sleep en route south to York. We didn't have to attempt to stay awake as the train terminated there and sure enough we were shaken awake upon arrival by the guard.

A photograph taken by window hanging out of the 08 20 Bradford Exchange to Bridlington shows Fairburn 42177 tackling the incline out of the terminus with the 08 20 parallel-timed portion departure for Wakefield (en route to Skegness). It was Saturday 2 July 1966 and often, during those summer Saturdays that year, the train crews co-ordinated their exits at photographers' behests.

A second shot of the Skegness service – the lighter train getting away to Bowling Junction the quickest. This Derby-built (1948) Fairburn tank 42177 escaped my clutches because on the day I was about to travel with her the train she was to work was cancelled due to a guard shortage! She was withdrawn from her home depot of Low Moor that December.

So here we were, on Saturday 2 July, at York at just gone four in the morning and our bleary eyes were rubbed clear to view the wonderful sight of a resplendent 45562 *Alberta* waiting at the head of the 04 35 departure for Leeds. Sleep deprivation was of little consequence when achieving catches such as this! After a trip over to Bradford Forster Square with Holbeck's 44828 on the normally DL-worked portion off of the 00 05 ex-St Pancras we had time to kill prior to the summer extras, which commenced shortly after 8 a.m. out of the Exchange station. We had planned to do a fill-in trip to Shipley and back, which upon reference to my notebook was crossed out, presumably being DL resourced. Some you win, some you lose! Walking over to Bradford Exchange we weren't certain that the 08 20 departure for Bridlington was steam worked and it wasn't until we could see at the head of the train the telltale safety valves lifting that we rushed over to the booking office for the necessary regulation and travel tickets. To say we were delighted to find Low Moor's 'pet' 45565 *Victoria* in charge would be an understatement. This departure, often synchronised at camera-equipped enthusiasts' requests with the parallel 08 20 portion for Wakefield, was a joy to window hang from. With three steam locomotives (our eight-coach train being assisted in the rear to Bowling Junction by Fairburn 42184) working their hardest, the noise reverberating off the incline's brick walls was music to a steam follower's ears.

It was time to settle down in the comfort of an uncrowded train and enjoy a 92-mile, three-and-a-half-hour journey by steam. So many of my catches in the NER area had been on short-haul services and it made a pleasant change not to worry about staying awake in readiness to alight at any intermediate stop. Having all the atmosphere of a rail tour this service was routed via Selby, the outskirts of Hull, Beverley and Driffield families stopping to stare at us, their children waving – the driver entering into the spirit of the occasion by hanging on *Victoria's* whistle at all level crossings and stations as we passed through the flat-landscaped vista. Some missed sleep from the previous night was caught up on, but I did note a max of 58mph through the Humber estuary village of Eastrington en route.

After arrival into the 120-year-old station at Bridlington, rather than retrace our steps we headed the 23 miles north to Scarborough, the largest holiday resort on the Yorkshire coast, passing the Filey Holiday Camp branch – built to serve the Butlin's Holiday Camp and lasting but 30 years (1947–77). On that day I again never ventured away from the station. I have, however, subsequently visited the town and being a fan of *The Royal*, the '60s themed hospital series, it would have been sacrilege to not seek out the cliff-side building where it was filmed, albeit the success being marred by wet and windy conditions of an English 'summer' August day.

In the early 1960s Scarborough station would have been awash with steam services on a summer Saturday but by 1966 just two departures remained – one of which, the 13 35 for Manchester, we had homed in on. Mirfield's 44694, piloted to York with Brush Type 4 D1542, was working the train on this day, resulting in another 40-odd miles of steam track being coloured in on my map upon my return home.

The 08 20 ex-Bradford Exchange after arrival at the East Coast resort of Bridlington on 2 July 1966. Low Moor 'pet' Jubilee 45565 *Victoria* (it was 56F's only Jub!) rests after her 92-mile journey – the 1934-built 6P5F being withdrawn in January 1967.

Alighting at Wakefield Kirkgate we now veered away temporarily from the NER by heading south to Sheffield, the reason being to cover the Hope Valley route on the steam-worked 11 55 (SO) Yarmouth Vauxhall to Manchester Victoria. This was the last of the twelve railway crossings built through the Pennines – opened as late as 1894 by the Midland Railway. Forged westward following the Derwent Valley via Edale, this scenic curvilinear route, which peaked opposite the infamous Snake Pass road so often blocked by snow during the winter, was certainly not built for speed. Having said that, the driver of our train that day for the 46¾ miles from Sheffield to Manchester, worked by Newton Heath's provision of 44846, knocked a seat-grabbing eighteen minutes off the schedule with some hair-raising speeds in the 70s and 80s on the way. Driver Fieldhouse's explanation upon arrival at Manchester was that he wanted to make the 18 35 for Oldham as his missus had his tea waiting! This early arrival fortuitously allowed us to backtrack over the Pennines, changing to, on paper a minus two-minute connection at Huddersfield, the 10 29 Poole/Bradford Exchange. The fortunate run of required locomotives petered out at this point – the eight-coach train being worked by 55C's 45647 *Sturdee* and double-headed in from Greetland Junction with Fairburn 42196.

As the reader might imagine, we were now beginning to tire and although we planned to catch the 22 00 one-coach departure for Huddersfield one of us (there was by now quite a gathering) had highlighted the fact that a 21 18 arrival (ex-Stockport) into Bradford Exchange was booked for a Low Moor tank. Wearily we traipsed out again to Halifax – some of the party required the incumbent 42055 – but not me! We finally

Extract from notebook.

departed the area courtesy of the aforementioned 22 00 Huddersfield service in charge of which was Bolton's 45304 – a locomotive allocated to a shed with no booked passenger work, making her very much required. During the week this train had a number of vans, which were conveyed forward westwards from Huddersfield on the TPO but on Saturdays it was comprised of just one brake standard corridor coach (BSK).

How, the reader might ask, did we make our way south at that time of night? Quite a few of us worked within various Train Planning organisations throughout BR and studying timetables was second nature to us. The York/Shrewsbury TPO (23 25 departure ex-Huddersfield) had two coaches detached at Stalybridge for Manchester Exchange, which, fortuitously on Sunday mornings only, was steam worked. This deposited us at Manchester at 00 26 conveniently connecting into the 01 00 Scottish sleeper's departure – worked to Wigan North Western by a Patricroft Standard 5. A one-and-a-half-hour fester there awaiting the southbound *Royal Highlander* would return us to London at 06 20, which, stamina permitting, allowed for a further 216 steam miles on a day trip to Bournemouth. On that particular weekend, having been out three nights and collecting a highly satisfactory 470 steam miles (250 on the NER) over rare routes (for steam) with nineteen different locomotives (six on the NER), not unsurprisingly I went home – now only requiring four Jubilees. If the above itinerary was a little complex to follow, please refer to Appendix V for the details in table form.

It was a lovely summer that year and somewhat fittingly the Kinks held the top spot for two weeks in July with *Sunny Afternoon*. On two Saturdays that month while travelling through the NER I didn't set foot there! On both occasions I was aboard the 21 20 (FO) St Pancras to Glasgow Central, which changed from a Peak DL to a Jubilee at Leeds City when reversing there. The first instance was on the 9th when 45593 *Kolhapur* took over at the 02 17/25 changeover and, having worked the 113 miles to Carlisle, was watered/re-crewed and worked forward the 116½ miles via the Glasgow & South Western (G&SW) route to Glasgow, presumably resulting from the booked replacement locomotive failing at Kingmoor. I had already earmarked that day for what turned out to be unsuccessful 'search and find' in the hunt for elusive V2 haulage in Scotland and the thirty-minute-late arrival into Glasgow caused no upset to the planned itinerary.

The second instance of travelling through the NER was on Saturday 30 July – a date etched into sporting history with England's 4-2 win over West Germany in the football World Cup. On this occasion Holbeck turned out 45697 *Achilles* which, although losing no further time en route, arrived into Carlisle at 07 23. The, by then, ninety-five-minute-late train having effectively kiboshed my planned Scottish bash, I abandoned ship heading south to the steam-infested Preston area. The reason for the delay was that at Chesterfield a drunken ATC put his arm through a carriage window resulting in a forty-five-minute delay, during which he was taken off the train by the local plod. A further forty-five minutes were lost at Sheffield while the coach concerned was taken out of the train – protracted shunting required due to its location in the centre.

Backtracking to 16 July once again (weren't we gluttons for punishment?), we commenced the 'day's' itinerary on the 02 00 ex-Sheffield – this time with a then required 45697 *Achilles*. After the Calder Valley mail train scenario (covered in the following chapter) we, George (a Scottish acquaintance met through our common interests) and I, changed off the 8L (I had to look that one up upon returning home – it turning out to be Aintree) allocated 44910-hauled 08 05 ex-Castleford at Brighouse onto the 09 08 Leeds City/Poole train worked to Huddersfield by Newton Heath's 44891. I read in *The Railway World* magazine some time later that this particular portion was worked on the final two Saturdays of its running that year by 42410, the last remaining Fowler tank on 27 August and LMS 8F 48267 on 3 September.

Oh well, you can't be everywhere at once! Anyway back to the 16th and I forget the reasons why we stuck to our original itinerary of a visit to North Wales with *Alberta*, working the 09 15 Leeds/Llandudno that day, but having witnessed 45581 *Bihar and Orissa* taking the Poole train forward to Nottingham and, with us both requiring her, we hastily revised plans to backtrack to Sheffield for her return working that evening. So off we went for a three-hour sojourn with *Alberta* – taking us over rarely used (by passenger trains) freight lines in the Manchester and Warrington areas – the fastest speed recorded on this rather tortuous 95-mile route being 62mph approaching Stalybridge.

Having had ample time to study the timetables at length, and being unable to make Llandudno due to late running, we alighted at Rhyl, catching Patricroft's Standard 5MT 73006 the 70 miles back into Manchester (at least the steam mileage was looking respectable that day!). It was a hot day and the walk between the Exchange and Piccadilly stations ended in a refreshing lager (no real ale railway outlets back then!) being supped in the station bar. We now had to recross the Pennines, via the Woodhead route, to Sheffield to connect with *Bihar*'s return working. Opened in 1845 by the Sheffield, Ashton-under-Lyne & Manchester Railway this was the fourth of an eventual twelve railway crossings over the Pennines.

At the time of construction the 3-mile Woodhead tunnel was one of the world's longest. Electrification, finally completed in 1955 using overhead 1,500 DC similar to the Dutch system, was, because of its uniqueness, its downfall. The cost of renewal or conversion to 25K proved uneconomic – passenger services ceasing in 1970 and freight lasting until the line's closure in 1981. Although used in the intervening years by the National Grid, reopening of the tunnels to rail traffic will, due to the lack of government funding, now never happen as a result of the November 2013 announcement that they are to be permanently sealed. Our locomotive on that day, EM2 Bo-Bo 27004 *Juno*, did, however, have an extension to her life, being purchased by the Dutch railways that used her until 1986.

Arriving into Sheffield's Victoria station at 17 59 we had but eleven minutes to spare (and tickets to be purchased) before *Bihar* departed the Midland station at 18 10. With coats and cases I am sure the shoppers never knew what hit them as we deftly circumnavigated around them in a panic-ridden rush across the city. One thing I am certain of all these years later is that the frequent walks/runs between stations at many cities and towns back then was contributory in avoiding possible obesity in later life. Just making it, after running down the steps as the 'right away' had been given, it was some minutes while recovering our breath before we began to appreciate *Bihar*'s effort at the front.

The first few miles had the novelty factor of steam 'under the wires', they being part of the Woodhead route, before heading north at Penistone over the Pennines via Denby Dale. Although sounding in fine fettle as she battled the gradients, this Farnley Junction-allocated Jubilee had but three weeks to go before withdrawal. Assisted into Bradford the final 10 miles from Greetland Junction, the bonus haulage with one of Low Moor's few remaining Stanier tanks just about rounded off a very successful day. Was that it then? Never missing an opportunity of an extra run if one could be fitted in we popped back to Halifax for a run in with the 19 30 ex-Stockport, completing, *Alberta* excepted, a run of ten required haulages.

The 22 00 one-coach Bradford Exchange to Huddersfield had, however, a surprise in store – Wakefield's B1 61224. She was in a poor condition, subsequently being withdrawn two weeks later, and somehow through either wet rails or grease slipped to a stand upon departure. Minutes ticked by and concern was mounting that a replacement

The 08 05 Castleford Central to Blackpool North, seen here prior to departure, on 23 July 1966 with Wakefield's 45739 *Ulster* – my final NER required Jubilee. Although I believe the train was booked for a 56A Jubilee, more often than not a returning LMR-allocated locomotive was sent out. This was the sixth locomotive of the Calder Valley 'circuit' (detailed in chapter 10) having started out at Sheffield six hours earlier. The 1936 Crewe-built *Ulster* was withdrawn in January 1967.

locomotive or substitute bus journey could jeopardise the connection into the westbound TPO at Huddersfield. If missed we would be stranded in the North East for the night. Concerns rescinded slightly as the driver skillfully coaxed his errant steed into action – the 21-mile journey being completed on time in the fifty-three minutes allowed, no doubt aided by the lax timings including a twelve-minute station stop at Halifax. Then it was back home, George and I parting company at Manchester after twenty-three hours together. That's how it was. Would our paths cross again? With the ever-decreasing availability of steam-hauled passenger services the likelihood was almost a certainty. As for my stats – just two more NER Jubilees to get!

Georgie Fame and the Blue Flames' *Get Away* had ousted the Kinks from the top spot by 23 July, and my last two required Jubilees fell into my lap on that Saturday. Starting off on the usual 02 00 departure out of Sheffield that morning, Holbeck had turned out 45675 *Hardy*. What a winner! Various events as detailed in the next chapter befell us that day, but on the 08 05 Castleford Central to Blackpool North the Wakefield foreman, perhaps following a failure of the normally LMR-allocated Black 5, turned out their 45739 *Ulster*.

Full of beans, literally after dining at the adjacent bus station canteen, I decided that I had blitzed the NER enough times over the past few weeks and, by changing at Mirfield, went across to Leeds for the 10 17 departure over Ais Gill to Carlisle. Once again *Kolhapur* took me over the Pennines although on this occasion I was to benefit from the glorious scenery missed while sleeping during the overnight travels so frequently undertaken previously. Perhaps here the opportunity presents itself for a brief history lesson about the line together with a description of the journey undertaken that day.

The 73-mile Settle to Carlisle line, the penultimate out of twelve Pennine crossings, was completed by the Midland Railway in 1876 consequentially from 'access' problems with the rival LNWR when forwarding their Scottish-bound passengers north of Ingleton over Shap. The line was constructed by a workforce upward of 6,000 mainly Irish navvies, lodging in shantytowns adjacent to the work sites, many of whom perished from the hazardous conditions they worked under. To this day, their graves are still tended by locals, some of whom are descendants of the original navvies. Using pickaxes and dynamite they hewed and blasted their way through the many rock faces over the Pennines, constructing twenty-two viaducts, including the impressive twenty-four arch one at Ribblehead, and fourteen tunnels. The Midland Railway had decreed the line to be built with as few speed restrictions as possible and, unlike the majority of railways constructed during those railway-mania days of the nineteenth century which followed river valleys and avoided hills, this route was one of the straightest – the resultant maximum 1-in-100 gradients over the 16 miles from Settle to Blea Moor earning the line the nickname of 'The Long Drag'. This decree in turn meant that any intermediate stations were often far from the villages/towns they purported to serve – an example being Dent, which was 4½ miles distant and 600ft higher than the village itself!

Returning to that July day, I took the opportunity, it being my first daytime visit over the route, of timing *Kolhapur* over the 113 miles from Leeds to Carlisle. Departing seven minutes late (10 24) nothing greater than 51½mph approaching Caverley was achieved over the 17¼ miles to our first stop at Keighley in twenty-six minutes, thirty-two seconds. With the gradient slightly less taxing, the 9 miles to Skipton, after being signal checked outside, were undertaken in just thirteen minutes, twenty-one seconds – maxing at 57mph approaching Cononley. The climb into the Northern Fells was beginning now and only the mid '40s were achieved in the seventeen-and-a-half-minute run over the 10¼ miles to our next stop of Hellifield. The remainder of the journey is detailed in the table below and, as can be noted, *Kolhapur's* low speeds reflect her struggle with the eight-coach train up the long climb up to Dent Head after which, although the fireman could rest a little and the driver having to be ever more vigilant, he could ease back on his exertions during the long descent. Window hanging, an essential practice for many a steam follower, just had to be undertaken during the thirty-minute climb to Dent Head. The annoyance of soot, grit and smuts was willingly endured in order to witness the sheer power, noise and visual effect of a steam locomotive working hard, her efforts resonating off the surrounding hills. All of this was enjoyed while passing through the spectacular scenery on offer. The terrain had become noticeably rugged with limestone outcrops now surrounding the green fields. Everywhere there were sheep. We climbed higher and nothing much seemed to separate us from an increasing expanse of sky of which, weather permitting, there was plenty of, the cloud formations being an artist's joy.

From a scenic point of view the line has much to recommend it and although the passenger benefits from the wildness of the Pennine countryside the weather makes a formidable enemy for the outdoor maintenance staff striving to keep the line open in the winter. To the west comes into view the black mass of Ingleborough with its curious flat top, on which, tradition has it, horse races were once held. Through Ribblehead station, dwarfed by the three peaks of Ingleborough, Whernside and Pen-y-Ghent, the line passes out onto the magnificent twenty-four-arched 100ft-high viaduct over Batty Moss. Straight up the valley from the west blow the westerly gales, and many a tarpaulin cover has been whipped off wagons as they cross this viaduct. Just prior to plunging into the 1½-mile-long Blea Moor tunnel a cluster of houses can be seen. With no approach road a small railway community once lived there – often isolated for days as the winter storms swept across the inhospitable moors. And so we dive into the inky darkness of the tunnel bored under the shoulder of Whernside and out into daylight. This is another world. Gone is the craggy bleakness, no longer the sound of hard labour from the locomotive.

We are at the top of the world – away to the west stretches the beautiful green valley of Dentdale. Then we pass through Dent station – England's highest at 1,150ft, where the owner of the holiday accomodation (the former station buildings) plans to open a fast-food outlet for train passengers who have pre-ordered their requirement at the previous calling point – into Rise Hill tunnel and over Garsdale water troughs. All around us are the Pennines – we are riding the backbone of England. We pass through Garsdale station, once known as Hawes Junction because of its NER connection across from Northallerton (via Stainmore), where in 1900 strong winds sent an engine spinning round uncontrollably on the turntable. To prevent a repetition, a stockade of vertically placed sleepers was erected around it. On Garsdale's platform is a statue of Ruswarp, the dog whose paw print was on the petition against the line's closure. He belonged to Graham Nuttel, a member of the Friends of the Settle-Carlisle Line, an organisation co-ordinating the fight against the line's closure in the 1980s. The dog was found still alive guarding his owner's body eleven weeks after his owner died whilst hill walking. Two short tunnels, Moorcock – the site of the 1910 train crash when the overnight St Pancras/Glasgow sleeping car train ran into two locomotives (signalman's error at Garsdale) killing twelve passengers – and Shotlock Hill, precede the summit of Ais Gill itself at 1,169ft above sea level as the line crosses the watershed into the Eden Valley and into what was Westmorland. On the right Mallerstang Edge dominates the scene until, passing through Birkett tunnel, the line enters open scenery. After passing through Kirkby Stephen West yet another closed (1962) NER line, between Darlington and

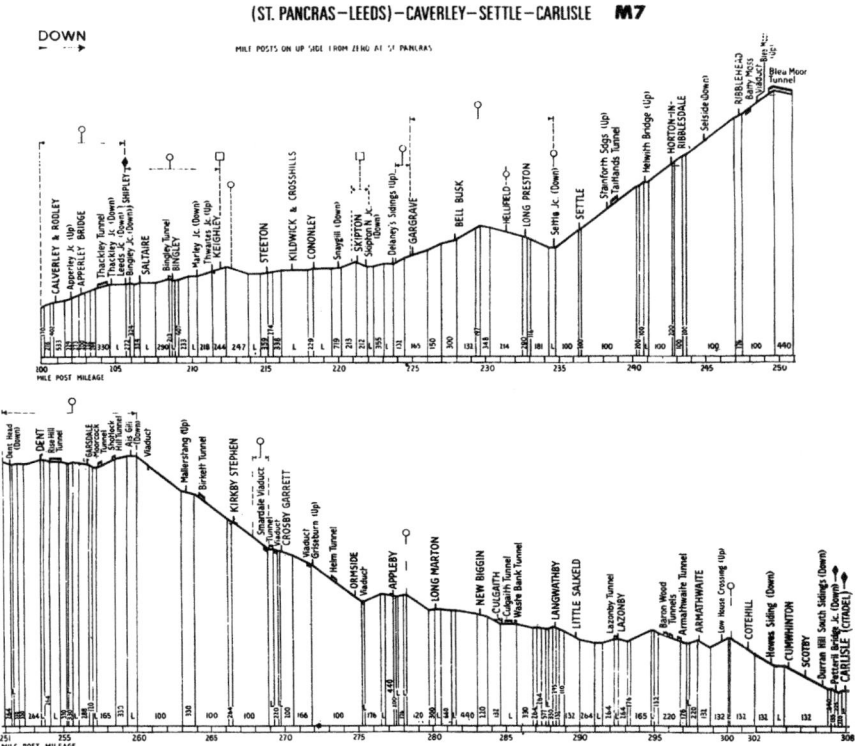

Gradient profile over 'The Long Drag'.

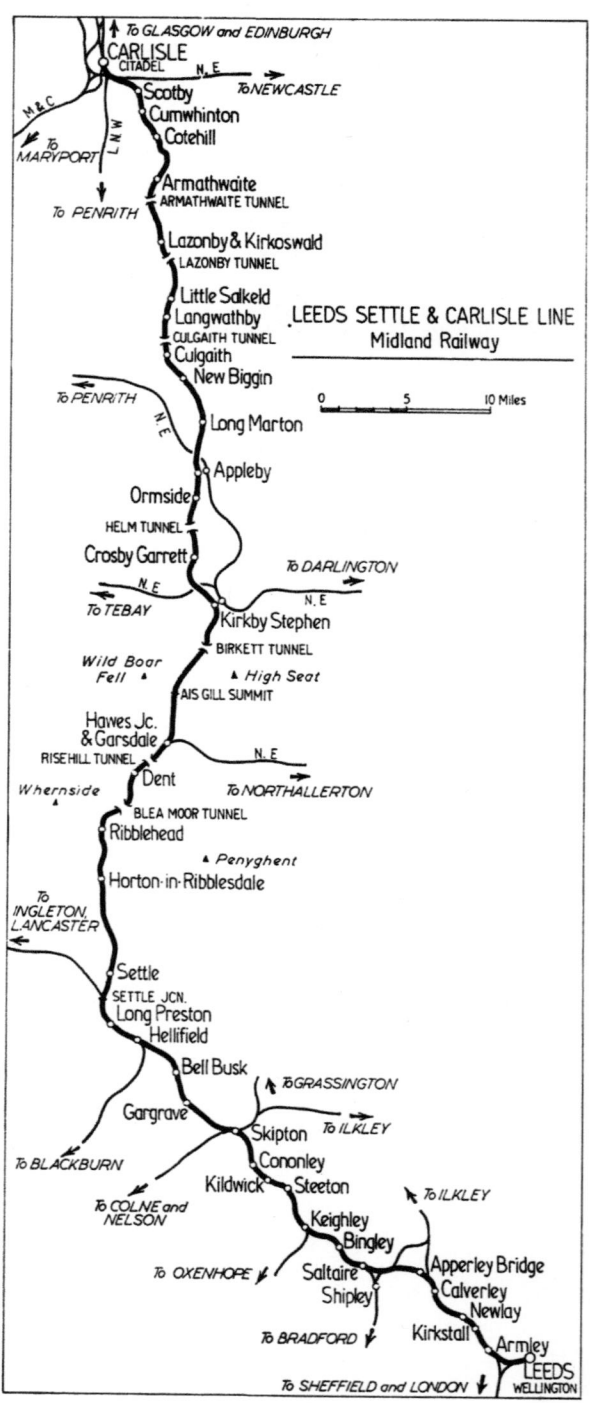

Map of the route (Ian Allan, *Trains Annual*, 1966).

Tebay via Stainmore, is crossed at Smardale, its twelve-arched viaduct at 130ft once being the highest on the Midland Railways system. A short breather is taken while calling at Appleby – well known for holding Britain's largest horse fair every June – where the connectional rails to the NER Eden Valley line are still in situ, albeit disused. We now enter the final stretch of the line with the lush green colours of the Eden Valley adorned with hamlets built out of local pink sandstone nestling in the crooks and crannies of the surrounding hills. The gradients all became downhill now, with speeds in the mid 60s and low 70s. It all had to end and after the arrival into Carlisle bang on time at 13 07 the remainder of that day was spent chasing steam south over the WCML.

Location	Time	Speed	Location	Time	Speed
Hellifield	00 00		Kirkby Stephen	50 54	70½
Long Preston	02 41	49	Ormside	58 35	62
Settle Junction	04 56	59	Appleby West	61 59	
	pws		Long Marton	04 41	56/60
Settle	07 28	33	New Biggin	08 03	63
Stainforth Sdgs	10 35	29½	Culgaith	09 17	67½
Helwith Bridge	16 14	30/35	Longwathby	12 24	70
Horton-in-R	19 12	28	Little Salkeld	13 42	73
Selside	24 00	29	Lazonby	16 04	68/71½
Ribblehead	28 53	30	Armathwaite	21 00	68/71½
Blea Moor	31 12	31/29	Howes Sdgs	25 38	56
Dent Head	35 52	52½/55	Cumwhinton	26 45	53
Dent	38 11	52/64	Scotby	28 07	56
Garsdale	41 36	62½	Petteril Bridge Jn	30 31	33
Ais Gill	44 44	58½	Carlisle	33 15	
Mallerstang	48 04	70/74			

After that day's captures the only active Jubilee remaining in Britain that I required was Bank Hall's (Liverpool) 45627 *Sierra Leone*, which, after a lot of false rumours, was eventually caught that September, just days before her withdrawal on a Blackpool/Liverpool service. By now the NER Jubilees had achieved celebrity status and whatever trains they worked were packed to the gunwales with enthusiasts and sightseers alike, creating an atmosphere more akin to rail tours. They had, rather like the pop stars of the '60s, achieved a cult following. Cleaned at their home depots by many 'unauthorised' hands (MNA?), photographs of the resultant iridescent locomotives working the summer Saturday trains out of Leeds and Bradford bound for east/west/south-coast resorts and Scotland have appeared many times over the years in the railway press.

Only three Jubilees survived into the summer of '67 and, with *Achilles* being withdrawn in early August, I was to enjoy just one run each with *Kolhapur* and *Alberta* – both on the 10 17 ex-Leeds (06 40 Birmingham/Glasgow). On 22 July, having earlier in the day departed from Sheffield on the 07 06 Leeds service (45428) I travelled with *Kolhapur* – a year to the day since my previous run. During the long wait at Leeds (the DL bringing the train from Birmingham had failed at Wath) and the glorious journey along the spine of England I had time to reflect on the past year's events.

So much had changed since then. The Kinks, who held celebrity status amongst SR enthusiasts with their *Waterloo Sunset* release commemorating the end of steam on the SR, highlighted the indisputable fact that we steam enthusiasts now knew for certain our hobby was coming to an end – but within such a short timescale? As a BR employee I was fortunate enough to enjoy free or reduced-rate travel – the only thing I was short of was time. I couldn't be everywhere at once so decisions and priorities had to be made as to where and what was most worthwhile chasing or being at. How opportune was I in being a young carefree teenager just at the 'right' time to catch Britain's final steam trains. Somehow escaping the NER steam cull that October,

Having travelled with *Achilles* out of Sheffield and over Ais Gill during the night hours I had no photographs from those occasions. On 29 April 1967, however, whilst en route from Leeds to Carlisle, an opportunity of a shot presented itself at Skipton where I was changing trains. A resplendent 45697 *Achilles* rests while working an afternoon Leeds-to-Morecambe van service – the 1936 Crewe-built Jubilee being withdrawn from her home depot of Holbeck four months later.

Where Are Those Elusive Jubilees?

Although most of my journeys made over the Long Drag were with NER-allocated Jubilees during 1966/67, the last occasion I travelled on a timetabled train was with a Britannia. On 29 August 1967 a relief to the *Thames Clyde Express* was worked by Kingmoor-allocated Britannia class 4-6-2 70004 *William Shakespeare*, seen awaiting her train from Glasgow. Fifty-five of these Riddles-designed 7P6Fs were built, this particular 1951-built example obtaining prestige status having worked the *Golden Arrow* between London and Dover for many years.

although both being withdrawn by the first week of November, only *Kolhapur* survived into preservation – three other former LMR-allocated Jubilees joining her.

Just one further concluding visit to the 'Long Drag' is worth detailing. It was in the August of 1967 – the month that saw the Beatles' *All You Need Is Love* knocked off the top spot by Bobbie Gentry's *Ode to Billie Joe*. The final bank holiday of each year was, until 1964, the first Monday of August. Starting from 1965 it was moved to the last Monday and taking into consideration it was the final weekend of the summer services – after which a great many steam services would cease running, I had earmarked it for a four-night bash. Although the main emphasis of chasing that weekend was centred on WCML services, I visited Leeds twice, travelled over both Shap and Ais Gill and caught an 'Adex' into Windemere before, on the Tuesday morning, finding myself at Preston at 8 a.m. in the morning.

Having already booked it as a day's annual leave I headed north for what I hoped was a possible steam-hauled daytime service over Ais Gill. While I had heard on the grapevine that the 09 56 *Thames Clyde Express* relief from Glasgow Central to St Pancras was booked for steam south of Carlisle, as always there was no guarantee. That there were no other enthusiasts on Carlisle platform led me to believe I had been hoodwinked!

O ye of little faith ... arriving into the centre road just prior to the eight-coach train itself the welcome sight of Brit 70004 *William Shakespeare* hove into view. This locomotive, which when new was displayed at the South Bank in London as part of the 1951 Festival of Britain celebrations as well as working the prestige *Golden Arrow* services for many years, then took me on the 113-mile journey over Britain's most scenic main line to Leeds, the timings of which I append below. It was a fitting finale, fortunately in wonderful sunny weather, to a wonderful weekend of steam.

Location	Time	Speed	Location	Time	Speed
Carlisle	00 00		Ais Gill	25 34	37½/63½
Petterill Bridge Jn	02 57	25	Garsdale	28 54	62½/58½
Durran Hill	03 58	35	Dent	32 15	60
Scotby	08 17	47	Dent Head	34 13	66½/67½
Low House Xing	14 03	60	Batty Moss	36 43	66½/71½
Armathwaite	15 40	56/60/56	Ribblehead	37 46	72½/80
Lazonby	21 10	66/67	Selside	39 43	77/73½
Little Salkeld	23 50	64/55½	Horton-in-R	41 31	75/80½
Langwathby	25 20	62/65½	Settle	47 12	
Culgaith	28 42	64/61½	Settle Junction	03 26	63
New Biggin	3002	62/58½	Long Preston	05 28	60
Long Marton	33 18	55/57	Hellifield	06 46	55
Appleby West	36 56		Bell Busk	11 11	64½/65½
Ormside	04 12	57½/45	Gargrave	13 54	63
Griseburn	07 48	39/42	Delaneys Sdg	15 06	61/62
Crosby Garrett	10 58	44/53/47	Skipton North Jn	17 00	59
Kirkby Stephen	14 58	41/35½	Skipton	18 14	
Mallerstang	20 10	39/42½			

I was exhausted. I stayed aboard the train, falling into a deep stupor south of Derby, being shaken awake by station staff upon arriving into St Pancras just gone 7 p.m. Was it all worth it? I'll leave you to make up your own minds with the following statistics from that final 1967 weekend of summer steam to mull over: twenty-six runs with twenty-two different locomotives (seven of which were required) – equalling 1,027 miles. Worth it? I should say so!

As regards the Settle-to-Carlisle line itself, during the 1970s the retrenchment-minded BR starved the route of investment – the condition of many viaducts and tunnels deteriorating accordingly. Using the 'closure by stealth' method often employed in those years, BR diverted freight services over the WCML and imposed draconian speed restrictions, causing increased journey times for the handful of trains still using it. In 1984 closure notices were posted. Many local authorities and rail enthusiasts joined forces, pointing out that BR was ignoring the S&C's potential for tourism and its usefulness as a diversionary route during occasions when engineering work or mishaps occurred on the WCML. The resultant publicity together with special 'Dalesrail' trains run for ramblers led to a huge increase in usage and BR appointed an outside consultancy in 1988 to advise on a 'possible sale'. The following year BR relented (the government's Michael Portillo of *Great British Railway Journeys* TV series fame taking the credit) and repaired the entire line's infrastructure 'faults', the route nowadays witnessing over a million passengers per year, together with forty freights per day.

10

Riding Yorkshire's Nocturnal Mail Trains

WITH MOST PASSENGER services on the North Eastern Region during 'normal' hours having, by 1966, gone DL/DMU-operated, a dedicated band of sleep-deprived haulage bashers were, by default, obliged to lead a nocturnal existence in order to pursue their hobby. It was only through chance conversations with like-minded enthusiasts that I was to discover a wonderful six-hour six-locomotive series of connections involving the Calder Valley mail services. This route via Hebden and Sowerby bridges was the third (of twelve) crossings over the Pennines being completed by the Manchester & Leeds Railway in 1841 – a company which became the major constituent of the Lancashire & Yorkshire Railway seven years later.

Although it had, by the summer of '66, become documented in various publications that the 02 00 Sheffield Midland to Leeds City was worked by a Holbeck locomotive, some of us (I include myself) were unaware that by alighting at Normanton at 02 52 we could connect into the steam-worked (from there) 02 10 York to Manchester Victoria departure a mere eighteen minutes later. This westbound train, having been brought the 24½ miles from York by a 'Long Pong', exchanged traction at Normanton for a Low Moor-allocated B1, which took the train the 22 miles to Halifax where, upon reversal, a Newton Heath-allocated Black 5 would take over. Sounds good – but it was to get better! If you, having struggled to stay awake through the sleep-inducing lengthy station stops en route, alighted at the Calder Valley station of Hebden Bridge you could, having waited a mere twenty-three minutes (05 05 to 05 28), catch the opposite way working – the 04 20 Manchester Victoria to York.

Hebden Bridge, a picturesque village set at the bottom of a deep valley surrounded by a lofty ridge of hillsides, has over recent years often hit the headlines as a result of frequent flooding from the River Calder and was another station where I never ventured away from the platforms. In this instance you can't blame me – it was the early hours of the morning! Overwhelmed by this regular volume of personal alighting there, the solitary railway porter's standard expression was 'you've all got rovers then?',

Table 21

York, Normanton, Leeds Central, Bradford Exchange, Halifax and Manchester Victoria

									E	
1 NEWCASTLE	d		23 14				..		..	
1 DARLINGTON	d		00 12							
YORK	d		02 10		04g35		•		•	
ULLESKELF	d	•					•		•	
CHURCH FENTON	d									
CASTLEFORD CENTRAL...	d	•	....		•		....	•	•	•
NORMANTON	a	•	02 48							
	d		03 10	04 25			•	07 01		
WAKEFIELD KIRKGATE	a	•	• 03 18	04 32				07 08		
2 LONDON KING'S CROSS	d		22A45	:.		..		01e15		
2 DONCASTER	d	•	01 58			..		06 30		
12 GOOLE	d		..				•	05 47	•	
19 BARNSLEY	d							06 10		
WAKEFIELD KIRKGATE	. d	•	03 36		•			07 12		..
HORBURY	d							07‡19		
MIRFIELD	a		03 52					07 28		
22 HUDDERSFIELD	a		06 54					07 42		—
22 HUDDERSFIELD	d							07 08		•
MIRFIELD	d		04 00		•	..		07 30		
BRIGHOUSE FOR RASTRICK	a		•		•			07 36	•	
	d							07 38	•	
28 HARROGATE	d	•				06 30	..		..	
LEEDS CENTRAL	d	03 10 03 32		..	06 21	07 13		•		0
ARMLEY MOOR...	d	•	•	..		07 18				0
BRAMLEY	d	•				07 22				0
STANNINGLEY	d	•		•	06 30	07 25	•			0
LAISTERDYKE ..	d	•		..		07 30		..	..	0
BRADFORD EXCHANGE	a	03 28	•		06 40	07 36		:.:		0
	d				06 47 07 25				07 45 07 50	
HALIFAX	a		03 59 04 26		06 59 07 37		..	08J13	07 57 08 02	
	d		04 38		07 04 07 39		•		07 58 08 05	
SOWERBY BRIDGE	• a		04 44		07 10 07 45			07 49	08 11	
	d		04 51		07 13 07 46			07 54	08 15	
MYTHOLMROYD	d		....		07 18			07 59	08 20	
HEBDEN BRIDGE	d		05 05		07 24 ..		•	08 04	08 27	
TODMORDEN ..	a		05 13		07 31 08 00	•		08 11	08 34	
	d	..	05 20		07 32 08 02			08 15	08 35	
LITTLEBOROUGH	d	•	....		07 38 08 08			08 22	08 41	•
ROCHDALE	a	•	05 34	•	07 44 08 14			08 29	• 08 47	
BOLTON ..	a	•	06 22		08 43			09 11	09k43	
ROCHDALE .	d		05 44		07 52 08 16		•	08 31	08 49	
MANCHESTER VICTORIA	a		06 00		08 11 08 33			08 48	09 04	•
BLACKPOOL SOUTH	a		07h55		10 17			11h06	11 06	
BLACKPOOL NORTH	a		07h55		....			11h06	• 11 06	
LIVERPOOL EXCHANGE	a		07h57		09 26			10h11	11j06	

Heavy figures denote through carriages;
light figures denote connecting services
For general notes see page 5

For complete service between York and
Church Fenton see Table 23
For other services between Normanton and
Wakefield Kirkgate, Table 19
Leeds, Manchester and Liverpool, Table 22

A Via Wakefield Westgate and Kirkgate.
   Passengers make their own way from one
   station to the other
C To Poole arr 19.14. Table 15
E To Stockport Edgeley arr. 09.05. Table 22
G 18 June to 27 August. To Bridlington arr 11.44.
   Table 10
J Change at Sowerby Bridge

The 02 10 York to Manchester Victoria westbound Calder Valley mail train timings.
This service was worked by a DL to Normanton and then steam (changing locomotives at
Halifax) forward. Most journeys were made boarding at Normanton at 03 10 and alighting at
Hebden Bridge at 05 05.

Table 21

Manchester Victoria, Halifax, Bradford Exchange, Leeds Central, Normanton and York

Miles	Miles									SO	B	SO	SO	SX
		LIVERPOOL EXCHANGE	d											
		BLACKPOOL NORTH	d											
		BLACKPOOL SOUTH	d											
—		**MANCHESTER VICTORIA**	d		**04 20**								**06 23**	
10½		**ROCHDALE**	a		**04 40**								**06 41**	
		BOLTON	d											
—		**ROCHDALE**	d		**04 49**								**06 46**	
13¾		LITTLEBOROUGH	d		**04 57**								**06 50**	
19		**TODMORDEN**	a		**05 09**								**06 58**	
			d		**05 14**								**07 02**	
23½		HEBDEN BRIDGE	d		**05 28**								**07 08**	
24¾		MYTHOLMROYD	d										**07 11**	
28½	—	SOWERBY BRIDGE	a		**05 36**								**07 16**	
			d		**05 40**			**06 56**					**07 20**	
	3¾	**HALIFAX**	a										**07 26**	
			d		*04n38*				**06 30**				**07 29**	
	11½	**BRADFORD EXCHANGE**	a						**06 42**				**07 41**	
			d	**05 35**			**06 23**		**06 50**	**07 20**		**07 40**		**07 45**
	13¾	LAISTERDYKE	d						**06 56**			**07 46**		**07 51**
	16¼	STANNINGLEY	d				**06 33**		**07 01**			**07 51**		**07 56**
	17½	BRAMLEY	d				**06 36**		**07 04**			**07 54**		**07 59**
	19¼	ARMLEY MOOR	d				**06 40**		**07 08**			**07 58**		**08 03**
	21¼	**LEEDS CENTRAL**	a	**05 53**			**06 45**		**07 13**	**07 37**		**08 03**		**08 08**
		28 HARROGATE	a	*06f43*			*07p42*		*08f27*					
34¼		BRIGHOUSE FOR RASTRICK	a		**05 49**			**07 04**						
			d		**05 53**			**07 05**						
38¼		MIRFIELD	a		**06 01**			**07 11**			**07 38**			
		22 HUDDERSFIELD	a		*06 54*			*07 42*						
		22 HUDDERSFIELD	d					*06 38*			**07 30**			
—		MIRFIELD	d		**06 10**			**07 12**			**07 39**			
43¾		HORBURY	d		**06‡20**			**07‡22**						
47¾		**WAKEFIELD KIRKGATE**	a		**06 30**			**07 29**			**07 53**			
		19 BARNSLEY	a		*07 50*						*08 51*			
		12 GOOLE	a								*09 25*			
		2 DONCASTER	a		*07 46*						*08g50*			
		2 LONDON KING'S CROSS	a								*10e45*			
		WAKEFIELD KIRKGATE	d		**06 42**			**07 32**						
50¾		**NORMANTON**	a		**06 50**			**07 39**			*08v20*			
			d		**07 06**									
54¼		CASTLEFORD CENTRAL	d		**07 15**									
64½		CHURCH FENTON	d		**07 32**									
66½		ULLESKELF	d		**07 36**									
75¼		**YORK**	a		**07 50**				*08f28*	*08f52*				
		1 DARLINGTON	a		*09 31*									
155¾		1 NEWCASTLE	a		*10 24*									

Heavy figures denote through carriages;
light figures denote connecting services
For general notes see page 5

For complete service between Church Fenton and York see Table 23
For other services between Liverpool, Manchester and Leeds see Table 22, Wakefield Kirkgate and Normanton, Table 19

B To Wakefield Westgate arr 07.59, Table 2
C Via Rochdale
E To Stockport Edgeley arr 09.05, Table 22
G Mondays to Fridays 25 July to 2 September. To Scarborough arr 11.01, Table 25
H Saturdays only

The 04 20 Manchester Victoria to York eastbound Calder Valley mail train timings. This service was steam worked throughout, changing locomotives at Normanton. Most journeys were made boarding at Hebden Bridge (05 28) and alighting at Normanton (06 50) if a DL took over, Castleford Central (07 15) when the dated Blackpool was running or York (07 50).

It's 5 a.m. on the morning of 2 June 1967 and Newton Heath's Black 5 Derby-built 44822 storms away from Rochdale with the 04 25 Manchester Victoria to York. I was LMR-based that day and after an hour's wait I caught sister 45083 back into Manchester on the 02 10 ex-York.

unaware that the more unscrupulous of us had filtered off down the approach road to refresh themselves with a pint of milk out of an unattended delivery. On several occasions we never made it that far, with mails and paper requirements sometimes taking longer than the booked allowances, timekeeping was not always adhered to. One of the more vigilant members of our entourage kept an eye on our progress and it was he who made the decision, kicking us awake or shaking our shoulders, to bale out a station short at Sowerby Bridge. Unlike Hebden Bridge, here officialdom was very much in evidence and they always attempted to check our ticket validity. Needless to say numerous ticketless enthusiasts melted into the dawn darkness, miraculously reappearing upon the eastbound train's arrival!

Although the eastbound train was Newton Heath-crewed the provision of power was random. Generally Newton Heath-allocated Black 5s were turned out, but there were weeks on end when either their Liverpool area or Holbeck-allocated sisters broke the monopoly. So now, during our one-and-a-half-hour journey to Normanton, we could attempt to regain some disturbed sleep – after all we had ahead of us a full day's chasing and energy had to be conserved!

Opened in 1840, Normanton was once a junction of three railways: the North Midland, the York and North Midland and the Manchester and Leeds, and, even after the 1923 grouping, retained two MPDs (LMS/LNER). Research led me to uncover a somewhat obscure fact about Normanton station. During the early days of the Midland Railway, a table d'hôte menu was handed out at St Pancras soon after a train, destined for Leeds, had departed. At Leicester orders were placed with the station staff who then telegraphed the diners' requirements to Normanton where the soup would be on the table as passengers poured into the dining room – just twenty minutes being allowed for the entire three courses to be consumed.

Returning to 1966, after arriving into Normanton at 06 50 the Manchester train was taken forward the 24½ miles to York by whatever was available. For us enthusiasts the variation was looked forward to in anticipation of 'something rare' – and we weren't disappointed. On the eight occasions I was aboard, the Normanton foreman turned out 50As B1s 61019, 61199 and 61319; 55As Black 5s 44857 and 45428 and his own Fairburns 42093 and 42149 and Ivatt 43043. A haulage is a haulage, however short the distance, and just nine minutes later, at Castleford Central, all us weary and hungry travellers alighted and fuelled our empty stomachs with copious quantities of beans on toast at the adjacent bus station canteen. Initially overwhelmed by the sudden surge in demand at that time of the morning the canteen manageress, over the coming weeks, became proficient in preparing vast quantities of beans prior to our arrival. Another first was the then novelty of somewhat fragile plastic knives and forks being provided. I say canteen rather than café, as I believe it should have been for bus crews only although we never had any problems getting served. They probably wanted the extra source of income! We had just fifty minutes for us all to be served because at 08 05 a summer Saturday train departed via Halifax and Copy Pit for Blackpool. This was the sixth catch and to this day I am unsure whether it was booked for one of Wakefield's two Jubilees or an LMR-resourced locomotive being returned west – more often than not it was the latter.

In my travels throughout those years all over Britain I was never able to surpass that six-hour six-locomotive itinerary for supply of haulages (although with careful planning the suburban services out of Paris Gare du Nord came a close second!) – nor I suggest did others. As an aside, I understand that with no one bothering to advise the

Normanton's Ivatt Mogul 43141 struggles to move a heavy freight at her home depot's yard on 23 July 1966 – the Doncaster-built 15-year-old being withdrawn that October.

The 46-year-old Armstrong Whitworth built 0-8-0 Q6 63420 runs light engine (LE) outside her home depot of Normanton on 31 August 1966 – being withdrawn in February 1967 at Tyne Dock.

The Newton Heath Black 5 had come off the 04 25 from Manchester Victoria here at Normanton and the foreman, always seemingly struggling to find adequate replacement power, supplied 19-year-old Doncaster-built B1 61019 *Nilghia* for the remaining 24½ miles to her home depot of York. The date was 27 August 1966 and she was to be withdrawn seven months hence.

canteen manageress that on Saturday 10 September and thereafter, when the summer dated 08 05 departure for Blackpool ceased to run, she was left with a great amount of cooked beans, there being no requirement to alight at Castleford ever again!

My first encounter of this scenario was on Saturday 16 July, a day after a controversial ban on black workers at Euston station was overturned, and all went to plan reaping runs with one Jubilee, two B1s and three Black 5s. The second attempt the following week, however, did not. The 02 00 from Sheffield, with 45675 *Hardy* at the helm, suffered a thirty-minute signal stand seemingly in the middle of nowhere en route to Normanton and the Manchester train was not held. There were twenty-eight enthusiasts present (a census was held on the Sheffield service during the delay) and having wandered around Normanton station we discovered that a BSK sitting in a bay platform formed a 04 25 for Rochdale (unadvertised beyond Wakefield), which we duly 'invaded' – at least it was out of the cold. In due course Wakefield-allocated Fairburn 42204 materialised out of the darkness, initially to provide welcome heat before then taking us the 3 miles to Wakefield Kirkgate where we changed onto the 05 15 to TV chat show host Michael Parkinson's hometown of Barnsley. None of us had ever caught this train before and the forty-odd minutes (04 32 to 05 15) spent loitering, in hope, at the deserted Wakefield Kirkgate station must have seemed, to an outsider, as a gathering of some cult organisation. You never knew what you were going to catch back then and on this occasion the earlier disappointment of missed trains now turned into elation. Yet another one-coach train was invaded and with

On 23 July 1966 the six-locomotive Calder Valley bash fell down because of late running (see text) and we (all twenty-eight of us!) ended up on the one-coach 05 15 Wakefield Kirkgate to Barnsley. Having run round her train, Wakefield's Flying Pig 43070 readies herself for the return 06 10 departure from Barnsley. She was to be transferred to Blyth from where withdrawal came in September 1967. (Alan (Nobby) Hayes)

Wakefield-allocated Ivatt 4MT Mogul 43070 (why did it have to be one that I'd had previously but new to all my mates?) in charge for the 11-mile journey I would think that the train never had been, or was ever again, so well patronised!

Luckily not being challenged by officialdom with respect to ticket validity during the thirty-minute turnaround the 'Flying Pig' duly returned us to Wakefield Kirkgate where, with just six minutes to wait, we picked up the 04 20 ex-Manchester and normality returned to our plans. I remembered afterwards that it had been detailed in Roger's book, but an isolated working, involving many hours festering on stations, not necessarily guaranteeing steam had been disregarded. As the summer of '66 wore on and word got around about this succession of catches the extraordinarily crowded scenes on these essentially mail trains, on which just one BSK was provided for passengers, had to be seen to be believed. The only method of securing one of the few seats on the westbound Manchester service at Normanton was to alight of the Sheffield train before it had come to a stand and race across the platform, a scene which surely in this day and age would have provided wonderful YouTube footage (it was after all at 3 a.m. when most sensible people were in bed!) – and only then sending one of the party up front to see what was to haul us on into the night! Slowly but surely the remaining locomotive numbers – those that weren't blacked out indicating withdrawal – in my Ian Allan ABC were no longer isolated redlined entries but several unbroken rows indicative of a seasoned traveller.

Although showing a 56D (Mirfield) smokebox shed plate I think Low Moor had already acquired Stanier 4-6-0 44694 as the *LCGB Bulletin* showed her being transferred there within weeks. The date was 31 August 1966 and she is seen at Bradford Exchange with the 15 05 portion for Wakefield.

After 23 July, having obtained runs with all the NER-allocated Jubilees, other parts of Britain were visited and it wasn't until the final Saturday in August that I was once again 'doing the circuit', having paid my last respects to the ex-GC route by arriving into Sheffield Victoria with Tyseley-allocated 44865 on the 19 15 ex-Swindon at a conveniently connecting 00 51 – into the 02 00 departure out of Sheffield Midland. I had deliberately caught this train because it was the only one covering the ex-GC route north of Nottingham (closing the following week) booked for steam traction. Having travelled out of the Midland station on the 02 00 departure it was nearly another miss at Normanton as the Sheffield train arrived into at 03 08 – just a two-minute connection!

Two more namers, B1s 61022 *Sassaby* and 61019 *Nilgai*, were caught on that particular occasion, and as some of the summer-dated services had ceased running, having partaken once again in the Castleford beanfest, I went over to the still steam-saturated LMR. Five days later, on Wednesday 31 August, saw the commencement of a five-

Extracts from my notebook.

nighter and after the aperitif of the Hebden Bridge bash one final concerted effort regarding services out of Bradford and Leeds was made. This involved a lot of toing and froing between the two Bradford termini of Forster Square and Exchange together with the Leeds counterparts of City and Central stations. I never noted where and when (cafes, station refreshment rooms, chippies?) my appetite was sated – Bradford had yet to receive the accolade of being the curry capital of Britain, that dish never being on offer back then. Much shoe leather and energy was used that day – monitoring as many arrivals and departures as feasible eventually yielded seven further 2-6-4Ts on the portion workings. This figure included one of the few remaining Stanier Tanks, 42622, and a Huddersfield Hillhouses (a shed without any booked passenger duties) allocated 42141 on *The Yorkshire Pullman* out of Bradford Exchange.

Thoroughly satisfied with my catches, I departed the NER once more on the 22 00 Bradford/Huddersfield continuing my pursuit of steam on the LMR on the final weekend of the summer-dated services that year. Spending the next three nights at Crewe, Preston and Wigan waiting rooms I was to eventually collect runs with forty-three different locomotives from nine classes totalling 983 miles – happy days! With the commencement of the winter timetable the 02 00 Sheffield went diesel and the Castleford/Blackpool ceased running – the never-to-be-repeated six in a row was now down to four.

11

ALL ABOARD THE RAIL TOURS

I WAS TO travel aboard a total of seven rail tours that traversed NER metals – details are as follows:

The Crab Commemorative Rail Tour – Saturday 8 October 1966

Riddles WD 8F 2-8-0 90076 – Wakefield Kirkgate (dep. 13 59) (via Applehurst Junction) to Goole = 32 miles.
LMS Hughes 5MT 2-6-0 42942 – Goole (via Knottingly) to Wakefield Kirkgate (arr. 17 11) = 27 miles.

This LCGB-organised tour originated at Liverpool Exchange and used representatives from two classes of steam locomotives I had never travelled with. Never working passenger services, one of Wakefield's 'Dub-dee's', 90076, worked the outward leg to Goole while 42942, one of the last surviving Birkenhead-allocated 'Crab's' returned the train westwards. A most rewarding hour or so was spent wandering around Goole shed photographing its allocation of WD 2-8-0s at close quarters – without the slightest interference from high-visibility-vest-wearing officialdom – no chance of that today! The day had started well with the Hebden Bridge bash (truncated at Sowerby Bridge due to late running) finishing with one of Normanton's Fairburn tanks, 42149, taking me into York – I never did get the other! After the tour's arrival back into Wakefield Kirkgate we walked over to the Westgate station where 56A turned out Bolton-allocated 44927 for the 18 25 portion to Bradford – the day being rounded off nicely with a 'namer' on the 22 00 for Huddersfield B1 in the form of 61030 *Nyala*. Six required locos, two new classes and loads of new track – could it get any better? (It did – 9D turned out a required 44845 for the 00 14 portion Stalybridge to Manchester Exchange on the way home!)

All Aboard the Rail Tours

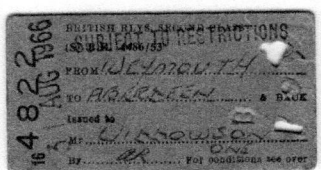
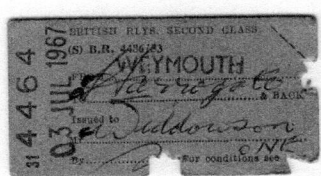
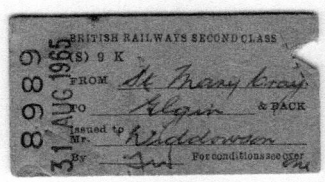
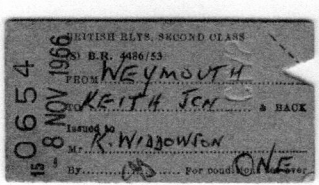
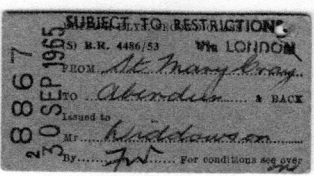

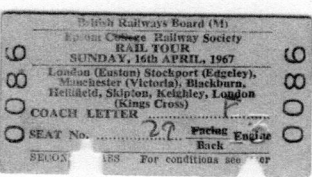
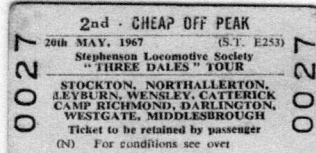
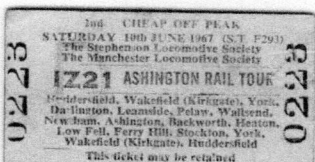

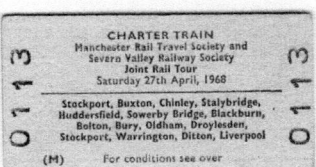

The rail-tour tickets and free passes used for my travels.

THE
LOCOMOTIVE CLUB OF GREAT BRITAIN

North West Branch

ITINERARY OF
THE CRAB
Commemorative
Rail Tour

SATURDAY, 8th OCTOBER, 1966

The front cover of The Crab Commemorative Rail Tour brochure – operated on Saturday 8 October 1966.

THE "CRAB" COMMEMORATIVE RAILTOUR

SATURDAY, OCTOBER 8th.

Liverpool Exchange (09.30)—North Mersey Jct.—Westwood Park—Manchester Vic. (pick up)—Accrington—Todmorden—Low Moor Avoider—Thornhill—Wakefield (change loco)—Hare Park Jct.—Stainforth—Goole.

Return from Goole direct via Knottingley—Wakefield—Mirfield—Rochdale to Manchester Vic. and Liverpool Exchange (20.30).

Motive Power: Liverpool—Wakefield and Goole—Liverpool; "CRAB" 2-6-0.
Wakefield—Goole: W.D. 2-8-0.

Fare: 40/- from Liverpool; 35/- from Manchester and 20/- from Wakefield. Accompanied Juveniles half fare. Buffet Car throughout.

Tickets and further details from:
R. L. HARDMAN, Esq., L.C.G.B. (North West),
12 HIGH BANK ROAD, PENDLEBURY MANCHESTER.

The September '66 *Railway World* advert for the tour.

A far from usual (i.e. spruced up!) WD 2-8-0 was used for the tour on 8 October 1966. Wakefield-allocated 90076 is seen at Goole having worked the tour the 32 miles from her home depot – she was to be transferred away from Wakefield upon that shed's closure in June 1967, to West Hartlepool, ending her days three months later.

We were able to wander at will in those far away days of non-health and safety around Goole depot and life-long resident WD 90094 was captured in camera.

An imposing view from ground level of Goole's 1943-built WD 90030 seen at rest – being withdrawn after twenty-four years' service in April 1967.

The celebrity, for which the tour was run, Hughes-designed Crewe-built 34-year-old LMS 42942, awaits the departure from Goole with the return trip to Liverpool. A total of 245 of these LMS 5F 'Crabs' were built but by October '66 a mere twelve remained – seven in the Ayrshire coalfield and five, including this one, at Birkenhead. She was one of the final two being withdrawn that December.

Extract from notebook.

The Mercian Rail Tour – Sunday 16 April 1967

E3103 Euston to Stockport Edgeley = 189½ miles.
LNER Gresley K4 6MT 2-6-0 3442 *The Great Marquess* (BR's 61994 – withdrawn in 1961) Stockport Edgeley to Leeds Central (via Manchester Victoria, Bolton Trinity Street, Blackburn, Colne, Skipton and Keighley) = 88¾ miles.
LMS Stanier 5MT 4-6-0 45377 (assistance) Bolton Trinity Street to Blackburn = 13¾ miles.
LMS Ivatt 2MT 2-6-2T 41241 (withdrawn December 1966) on Haworth branch = 4 miles.
LNER Gresley 8P A3 4-6-2 4472 (BR's 60103 – withdrawn January 1963) Leeds Central to Kings Cross (arr. 21 58) = 185¾ miles.

This Epsom Railway Society-sponsored rail tour used three preserved steam locomotives – Viscount Garnock's K4 3442, the embryonic Keighley & Worth Valley Railway's (K&WVR) Mickey Tank 41241 and Alan Pegler's 4472. It had been planned that a trip over K&WVR metals would take place, but the necessary Light Railway Order had yet to be granted. We were all bussed from Keighley to/from Haworth where a 4-mile 'shunt' along what was available took place. I also 'cabbed' the star of *The Railway Children* film – 80-year-old Lancashire & Yorkshire (L&Y) 0-6-0 Ironclad 957. Originally shown

A mere five LNER 6MT 2-6-0 Gresley-designed K4s were built. Here, at Blackburn on 16 April 1967, the now privately-owned 1938 Darlington-built 6MT 61994 (painted up with her LNER number of 3442) *The Great Marquess*, withdrawn at Thornton Junction in 1961, readies herself for the haul over Copy Pit en route to Leeds.

The Mercian organisers had advertised a run over the embryonic Keighley & Worth Valley Railway, but the necessary Light Railway Order hadn't been authorised by the date of the tour. The participants were therefore bussed to Haworth where 'Mickey Tank' 41241, withdrawn at Skipton the previous December, shuttled us along what was available. A total of 130 of these Ivatt-designed 2-6-2T locomotives were built and distributed throughout all the regions of BR – this one fortunately surviving into preservation. Here we see her on a visit to *The Watercress Line* in Hampshire where, coupled with sister 41312, she departs from Ropley on 13 September 2008.

to travel via Leeds City and change locomotives at Wakefield, the changeover between the K4 and the A3 actually took place at the soon-to-be-closed Leeds Central. Another two classes of steam locomotives were scratched!

The Three Dales Rail Tour – Saturday 20 May 1967

BR Peppercorn K1 6MT 2-6-0 – Stockton (dep. 10 17) via Northallerton, Redmire, Catterick Camp and Richmond to Darlington (arr. 15 50) = 112¼ miles. Top and tailed with Sulzer Type 2 D5160 – Northallerton (via Redmire) to Darlington = 58¼ miles.

Yorkshire was by this date becoming a desert for both steam followers and football followers alike in 1967. The Bradford portions had ceased that April, the FA Cup being played out by two London clubs (Tottenham 2 Chelsea 1) and the four division championships being won by Manchester United, Coventry City, Queens Park Rangers and Stockport County respectively. The one highlight, for the former, was this Stephenson Locomotive Society organised tour utilising 62005, one of the half-dozen remaining K1s. Formed of just six vehicles I thoroughly enjoyed the near six-hour tour that travelled over many freight-only branches, and with speeds never exceeding 40mph I had ample opportunity for viewing the picturesque Dales – the highlight being, perhaps, a circuit around the Catterick Camp Military Railway. Prior to the rail tour I had naturally partaken of the Hebden Bridge aperitif of steam after which, when passing through York en route to Stockton to pick up the tour, I espied one of the twenty-strong class of BR 2-6-0 3MTs, 77012 outside the shed – together with several condemned B1s. By alighting at Darlington in the afternoon and travelling over to Carlisle, I rounded off the weekend with 73 miles of Brit 'fix' into Scotland. Recommended background reading on organising a rail tour such as this can be viewed on the North Eastern Locomotive Preservation Group's website (www.nelpg.org.uk) where a 'Memories of the Day' article by Maurice Burns details the traumas and difficulties in securing the necessary authorisation to operate over lines no longer catering for steam locomotives.

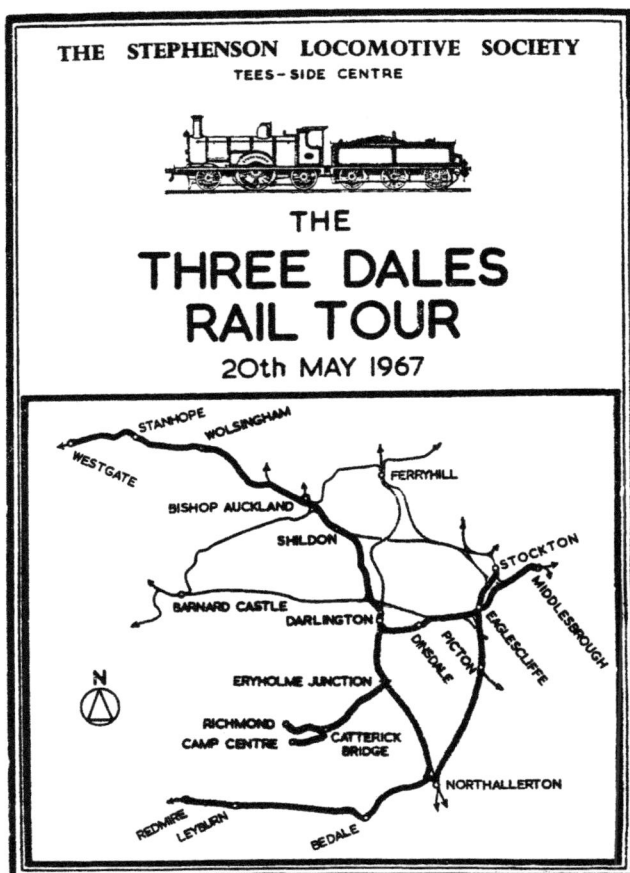

The front cover of the Three Dales Rail Tour pamphlet – operated on Saturday 20 May 1967.

Attention back there! Having just completed a circuit of the Catterick Military railway, Blyth-allocated K1 62005 is seen at the photographic stop of Catterick Bridge while working The Three Dales Rail Tour on 20 May 1967. This 1949-built K1 was the very last steam locomotive to be withdrawn on the NER (at Holbeck in December 1967) having been selected for preservation.

Here we see K1 62005 coupled with Sulzer Type 2 D5160, provided for top-and-tailing purposes to avoid numerous run rounds at the various termini, at Redmire – the truncated terminus of the route over the Pennines to Garsdale née Hawes Junction. Redmire, having lost its passenger services way back in 1954, reopened in 2004 courtesy of the Wensleydale Railway preservationists who run trains over the 18-mile section to Northallerton West.

Another scene from the Three Dales Rail Tour sees the K1 Mogul at the subsequently conserved station of Richmond (albeit as a cinema/heritage centre) – the Beeching axe ensuring that it was to lose its services in 1969.

The Ashington Rail Tour – Saturday 10 June 1967

LMS Stanier 5MT 4-6-0 45428 Wakefield Kirkgate (dep. 08 57) to York = 27½ miles.
LMS 6P5F Jubilee 45562 *Alberta* York (via Leamside, Newcastle and Percy Main) to Ashington = 102¼ miles.
NCB 0-6-0ST 39 Ashington Colliery circuit = 4 miles.
45562 *Alberta* Ashington (via Heaton, Newcastle, & Stockton) to York = 103½ miles.
45428 York to Wakefield Kirkgate (arr. 21 26) = 27½ miles.

This was a jointly organised tour between the SLS and the Manchester Locomotive Society. Ex-Farnley Junction Black 5 45428 had become a Holbeck 'pet' during the final months of NER steam and was turned out polished to the nines. *Alberta* was similarly treated and with only four Jubilees remaining any run with one was worth the effort. The northbound route, via Leamside, was that of the original East Coast route – superseded in 1872 when the more direct route that we nowadays know as the present ECML was opened. This route, having lost its passenger services in 1964, was mothballed in 1991 and is currently being considered for reopening, the ECML expected to reach capacity point by 2018.

The novelty trip around the Ashington colliery (the unofficial capital of the Northumbrian coalfield) was temporarily marred by the loss of my spectacles – they being posted to my home a week later by considerate officials at the National Coal Board. Procol Harum's *A Whiter Shade of Pale* was topping the charts back then and, as a novel way of keeping awake during the obligatory Hebden Bridge bash undertaken during the early hours of that day, strains of 'skipped the light fandango' were to be heard!

Upon arrival into Normanton 61388 was backed onto the 04 25 ex-Manchester to take the train forward to York. Always grateful for a run with a B1, I have to say that when she was failed by the driver and replaced with Holbeck's 44857 I was selfishly pleased. Why so? I had already had a run with the B1 – but not with the Black 5!

Although the tour started and finished at Huddersfield, by alighting at Wakefield Kirkgate on the return journey, a 14½-mile run with a required Low Moor-allocated 42252, she having been displaced at Tebay by the influx of BR 4MT 75xxxs, was enjoyed to Huddersfield on the once-a-day unusually routed 22 04 portion to Bradford (via Huddersfield/Halifax). Was that the end of my travels that weekend? With the cessation of SR steam fast approaching I think not – a day trip to Bournemouth being enjoyed and finally reaching home after fifty-four hours on the go.

The Ashington Rail Tour on Saturday 10 June 1967 had Holbeck-allocated Black 5 45428 working the train from Wakefield Kirkgate to here at York. This ex-Farnley Junction Black 5 had worked the Royal train to Nidd Bridge the previous month and was subsequently sent out on all prestige duties – surviving until the NER cull that October.

The incongruous mix of an express steam locomotive in coal siding! Having brought the tour the 102 miles down the ECML and through Newcastle, 45562 *Alberta* is seen at the NCB colliery of Ashington.

The Northumbrian colliery of Ashington on 10 June 1967 and NCB 0-6-0ST 39 readies herself for a 4-mile circuit of the coal mine's railway system. The comparison of the 'comfortable' BR Mark 1 coaching stock with the single compartmented miners' accommodation can be easily seen.

Similar to Goole the previous year we were able to wander freely throughout the complex. Here 0-6-0ST 3 contains a full footplate with three of my travelling friends from those halcyon days – Andrew (Clackers) Clarke, Graham (Jock) Aitken and Bob (Doze) Thompson. Whether we liked it or not we were all given nicknames; mine, because of my large sideboards and occasional moustache, was Keith (Wild Bill) Widdowson as I was being likened to the American cowboy lawman/gunfighter Wild Bill Hickok.

The Preservation Special – Saturday 28 October 1967

LMS Stanier 5MT 4-6-0 45411 Stockport Edgeley (dep. 11 20) to Manchester Victoria = 7 miles.
Riddles BR 7P6F 4-6-2 Britannia 70013 *Oliver Cromwell* Manchester Victoria (via Hebden Bridge, Penistone, Sheffield Victoria & Doncaster) to Normanton = 117 miles.
LMS Stanier 6P5F Jubilee 45562 *Alberta* Normanton (via Halifax & New Pudsey) to Normanton = 47¾ miles.
70013 *Oliver Cromwell* Normanton (via Kirkstall & Skipton) to Rose Grove = 54½ miles.
Riddles BR 5MT 4-6-0 73040 Rose Grove (via Blackburn) to Manchester Victoria (arr. 21 38) = 34¼ miles.

Although no photographs were taken whilst aboard the Preservation Special of 28 October 1967, I had travelled with one of the locomotives used on the day, Britannia 70013 *Oliver Cromwell*, thirteen days earlier. Selected for eventual preservation, she is seen taking water at Hellifield while working the Kingmoor Rail Tour on 15 October 1967.

This jointly organised tour (Severn Valley Railway Society/Manchester Rail Travel Society) started and finished at Birmingham New Street. All steam locomotives barring Jubilee 45562 *Alberta*, K1 62005 and a dozen or so 8Fs at Royston had gone from the NER by this date and I was aboard this tour possibly lured by the original booking of an 8F on the circular routing of the train through West Riding. No notes were made at the time as my disappointment/joy of once again having a final run with *Alberta* — in place of a guaranteed required 8F! She hadn't been used for three weeks (having been stored at Holbeck) and was to be withdrawn seven days later.

A4 to Edinburgh – Saturday 4 November 1967

LNER Gresley 8P 4-6-2 60019 *Bittern* Leeds (dep. 08 45) to Edinburgh (arr. 13 34) = 230¼ miles.

Having let go the A3 at Newcastle in August '64 on an Edinburgh train the massive void of ECML track over which I hadn't covered with steam was sated on this day by this rail tour organised by The Railway Correspondence & Travel Society (RCTS). *Bittern* had been withdrawn at Aberdeen in September 1966 and was privately preserved, being owned by Geoff Drury. I had covered the Calder

All Aboard the Rail Tours

With the last of the class being withdrawn in Scotland the previous summer the now privately owned A4 60019 *Bittern* was used on The A4 to Edinburgh Rail Tour on Saturday 4 November 1967 – seen here at Newcastle. She was one of thirty-four Doncaster-built LNER Gresley-designed 4-6-2 Pacifics used on the crack expresses over the ECML, one of which, *Mallard*, holds the world record for the fastest recorded speed with a steam locomotive: 126½mph. Most of the class were equipped with corridor tenders thus allowing the crew to change over without stopping. It was this very platform, readers might recall, that three and a half years previously I had failed to appreciate the significance of travelling with steam over the Scottish border by letting A3 60112 *St Simon* head north without me aboard – an error rectified this day.

Valley services for the first time since the 1 October cull, catching just one steam, the 03 32 Leeds/Halifax/Hebden Bridge (a non-required 9D-allocated 45203 to boot!), the eastbound mails having gone diesel. After the tour I returned south, travelling over the wonderfully scenic 98¼-mile Waverley route, to Carlisle. Since the winter timetable change that September there were no booked regular steam passenger services over Shap, or indeed would ever be, and it wasn't until arrival that evening into Preston that my steam-starved day improved – catching the subsequently preserved 'Flying Pig' 43106 on a Blackpool portion.

Preservation Special No. 2 – Saturday 27 April 1968

As this was my very last steam incursion into BR's Eastern (née North Eastern) Region I have included the details within the final chapter (15).

12

BRIEF ENCOUNTERS

NO THIS CHAPTER isn't about Carnforth, the scene of the *Brief Encounter* film – my exploits over the WCML are held over for another book! Having completed the task set by myself of catching runs with all of the NER Jubilees quicker than anticipated, 23 July 1966, my interest in the West Riding steam scene waned somewhat. That summer was spent predominantly living on steam trains the length and breadth of Britain. At just over 35,000 steam miles 1966 was to prove my highest yearly total ever. Whilst admitting about a half of that was on SR metals, considerably assisted by holding a 'privilege' season ticket between London and Southampton, the LMR's WCML steam services provided a healthy contribution. That area thus became the draw for the remainder of that summer – hunting down and catching runs with the remaining required Britannias being my next mission. I did, however, make occasional 'brief encounters' over the NER, as follows.

Until the November of 1966 a somewhat unique working of a Low Moor tank was diagrammed to work the three-coach 15 20 Bradford Exchange to Stockport Edgeley – together with the balancing 19 35 return. The westbound train called at Halifax, Brighouse, Huddersfield and Stalybridge. The eastbound evening working, while calling at all the above, also had set-down only stops at Saddleworth, Marsden, Slaithwaite, Golcar and Longwood – 'for passengers from south of Crewe upon notice given to the guard at Stockport'. Although having sometimes, after a long day bashing in West Riding, often boarded the return working at Halifax, it wasn't until 3 September when, at the end of a four-nighter, I caught the 45-mile journey in its entirety with one of the seemingly two regular Fairburns used on the train – 42116. Ominously my returning one-coach train, the 22 00 Bradford/Huddersfield, was (over) powered by English Electric Type 3 D271 – was this yet another train gone over to DL operation, I wondered at the time? Fortunately, as can be noted further on in this chapter, it appeared to have been a one-off. The novelty, to me, of a tank locomotive journey over the Pennines was thoroughly enjoyed and, having ascertained that a not-required Brit (70010) was booked out of Crewe on the 18 25 Barrow departure some seven weeks later I repeated the itinerary – on that occasion with 56F's 42184.

Upon arrival into Bradford that evening I was presented with a dilemma. The 21 25 Wakefield portion had 56A's B1 61123 on it – the 22 00 Huddersfield had 45197 on it. I required both and the persuasive factor in taking the 22 00 option was that had I gone with the B1 I would have arrived into Kings Cross at the unearthly hour of 03 26 – the prospect of a walk across London (before any transport had started up) failing to appeal to a weary traveller. By taking the 22 00 and connecting into the Manchester portion off of the TPO together with a Standard Caprotti on the sleepers coupled with a more sociable arrival into London at 06 20 was enough to sway me to that alternative. Although, figuratively speaking I made the correct decision at the time (catching three requirements vice one en route home) I lost out on the B1. I was never destined to have a run with her – she being transferred to York weeks later and withdrawn the following May.

Two weeks later, on 5 November – the Four Tops having knocked Jim Reeves' *Distant Drums* off the top spot with their *Reach Out I'll be There*, a repeat scenario, i.e. Brit 10 on the Barrow – saw me once again making my way to Stockport for a third occasion. Starting away from Stockport over the lengthy twenty-seven-arched viaduct straddling the ex-Cheshire Line Committee's Tiviot Dale line the first half mile, to Heaton Norris, was uniquely 'under the wires'. After then, having negotiated our way through the many eastern Mancunian suburbs to Stalybridge, the journey really took off. This crossing of the Pennines was the fifth, out of twelve, and was completed by the LNWR in 1848. Ascending the 1-in-125 incline towards the infamous Saddleworth Moor, the rugged limestone ridge prominent in the night sky, for nearly

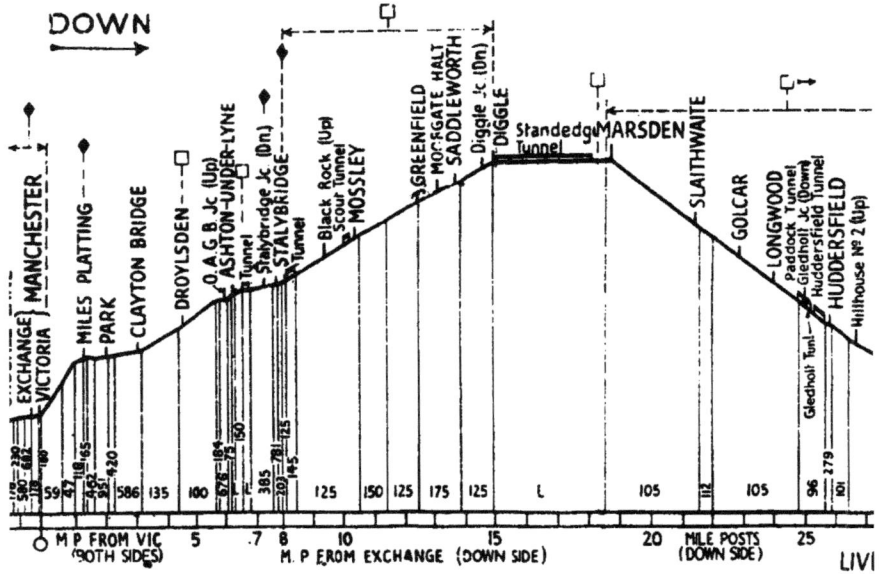

Gradient profile over the Pennines – Stalybridge to Huddersfield.

2 miles the Fairburn tank certainly let all nearby know she was coming – her exhaust resonating off the hillsides. With many of the occupants of the clusters of houses that nestled in the hollows at the foot of these hills celebrating Guy Fawkes Night – the smoke and glow from a great number of bonfires, together with the rockets/debris being sent up into the sky, harmonised aptly with 42116's (again!) exertions.

All the main arteries of communication – road, river, canal – ran side by side through the textile townships en route. Magnificent cotton mills, often described as dark and satanic, loomed out of the blackness – as a reminder to the passer-by of the inhabitants' contribution to the industrial revolution. You had to have been there to witness the scene: reflections of the tank's fire in her billowing ear-splitting exhaust being observed from the obligatory window-hanging position in the leading coach.

Storming away from the station stops on and on she climbed, eventually after nearly 7 gruelling miles, entering the second longest tunnel through the Pennines – that of the 3-mile 60-yard-long Standedge tunnel. Only then could I sit back and wipe the smut and grit off my face, luckily on this occasion not getting anything in my eyes. Exiting the tunnel at Marsden it was downhill the 7 miles into Huddersfield – both of us (enthusiast and crew) no doubt suffering from partial hearing loss. In this hobby of mine you sometimes chance across being in the right place at the right time and I was completely unaware that it was the last occasion – the train going DMU the following Monday. It was utterly memorable and rounded off by recently reallocated, ex-Trafford Park, Stanier tank 42574 returning me to Huddersfield on the (as ever) conveniently connecting 22 00 departure. This train, a service upon which I relied to exit from Yorkshire homeward-bound on many an occasion, didn't appear in the following year's timetable – presumably being either vans only or completely cancelled.

The following year, having concentrated on the demise of SR steam until the July, the majority of the summer was once again spent on LMR metals. On one particular July Sunday morning, having jumped aboard a double-headed Black 5 powered Paignton/Glasgow 'adex' at Wigan, assuming it called at Preston, I found myself effectively stranded at Carlisle (its first stop!) at 03 30 in the morning. With no trains back south for many hours and the adex having been taken forward by DL, rescue came, albeit one-and-a-half hours later, in the form of Brit 70024 *Venus*. At 5 a.m. she took over a relief ex-St Pancras via the G&SW route and Dalry the 127 miles to Glasgow. It was a gloriously sunny Sunday morning and although taking me in the opposite direction to that intended, because by then steam incursions over the border were becoming rare, I sat back and enjoyed the moment. So after arrival into Glasgow Central at 08 08, and having missed a southbound WCML service back to the smoke, after a hurried perusal of the ever-present saltire-blue-covered Scottish timetable (no wonder my case was always heavy!) I surmised the quickest way south was to walk over to Glasgow's Queen Street station and head to Edinburgh for the 10 00 Kings Cross departure via the ECML – hence the inclusion of this journey in a book about the NER! What a wonderful trip that train turned out to be. With Deltic D9017

The Durham Light Infantry in charge a right-time departure was made but, resulting from a derailment at the Northumbrian station of Ackington, we were diverted over the Waverley route via Hawick to Carlisle then on via Hexham – regaining the booked route at Newcastle. Not having had anything to sate my hunger over the preceding twenty-four hours, I was famished and, after counting my pennies, treated myself to a meal in the restaurant car. As for timekeeping the eventual 427-mile journey, no doubt resulting from lax Sunday schedules, brought me into Kings Cross a mere sixty-one minutes late at 18 11 hours.

The next brief encounter was on Friday 18 August when, perhaps having viewed a common, i.e. not required Carnforth Black 5 on the 20 55 *Belfast Boat Express* departure out of Manchester Victoria, we caught the 21 05 Trans-Pennine service over to Huddersfield, connecting with the 22 33 for Bradford Exchange – worked that night by Low Moor's 42141. This was a portion off the 18 53 ex-Kings Cross that had been detached at Wakefield Kirkgate and routed via Huddersfield and Halifax – and was running over half an hour late. Having noted the recently transferred (from Hull Dairycoates) B1 61306 while passing the now recoded Low Moor shed (55J), we arrived into Bradford Exchange at 23 46. After a minor altercation, the ticket barrier staff who, upon viewing our Weymouth-to-Perth free passes, stressed the fact we were well off route, escorted us onto the 23 55 Kings Cross departure – the very train we were planning to catch anyway. We had pleaded ignorance of the portion working and promised to continue our journey to Perth from Doncaster. Black 5 44694 worked this Friday-only dated train the 9½ miles to Leeds City – from where English Electric Type 4 D348 took over. We (Jock and I) had fallen asleep on that short run and, suddenly awakened by some sixth sense while at the Doncaster station stop, I jumped off not realising Jock hadn't! As I stood on the platform viewing my sleeping friend stretched out in the warm compartment (SR malachite green liveried S855 for those coaching-stock aficionados!) I was never going to let him sleep on to London, a trick sometimes played on fellow 'unliked' companions by any one of us (it wasn't just me!), and after some vigorous thumping on the window a startled Jock joined me outside.

Deltic D9013 *The Black Watch* took us back north depositing us at 02 18 at the deserted and partially derelict Wakefield Kirkgate station where we festered for one and a half hours awaiting the York/Manchester mail train. The night was to get worse because, upon the train's arrival, instead of the expected steam locomotive, Type 3 'tractor' D6947 (transferred in from Wales at the recently opened nearby diesel depot at Healey Mills) was in charge. To compound the disastrous night an extremely common Newton Heath 45203 took over at Halifax. You sometimes wondered if it was all worth it, but fortunately matters improved later that day when visits to Morecambe, Kendal and Blackpool all delivered required steam!

I was to reenact a similar scenario two weeks later, on this occasion, however, arriving into Leeds on the 17 47 Manchester Exchange/York working. Crossing over to Bradford for the 20 45 Fridays-only dated Paignton train ex-Mirfield 45208 took us back over to Leeds. Staying aboard we alighted at Wakefield for the portion, which two weeks previously was the focus of the confrontational scene upon arrival into Bradford and the locomotive that was to perform the 'last rites' the following month – Fairburn 42152. Luckily the scene wasn't repeated and we once more caught the 23 55 departure – unbelievably 45208 having run light engine back from Leeds to work.

Once more repeating the cycle of trains caught two weeks previously, we went south to Doncaster and north-west to Wakefield for yet more twilight hours spent festering there for the westbound Calder Valley mails. The reader might wonder about the mentality of such moves in the middle of the night, when barring shift workers, most normal persons were tucked up in a warm bed. As a vindication I can only state that it was all disappearing and it had to be done. I can look back into my notebooks and records with gratifying satisfaction in that nothing like the scenario viewed and participated in back then can be replicated nowadays – the sleep deprivation, cold and festering for many hours not, as yet, appearing to have had any detrimental effect on my longevity! Although this brief encounter didn't reap any new catches at least the trains that should have been steam were.

13

No More Wakefield Portions

ALTHOUGH THE NORTH Eastern Region had been amalgamated within the Eastern Region of British Rail since 1 January 1967, the HQ being located at York with the redoubtable G.F. Fiennes as the General Manager, BR continued to publish a separate 228-page public timetable – as before contained within its distinctive tangerine-coloured covers. Although denoting validity from 6 March until 3 September, on delving inside it showed Leeds Central having been expurgated from it – a note on the relevant pages (tables 19 and 21) reading 'Important. The services printed above operate from 1 May 1967. For services 6 March to 30 April see separate supplement' – the tables concerned underscoring the fact that Bradford Forster Square had lost all of its 'portioned' trains to and from Leeds City.

Leeds Central railway station, opened in 1854 as a joint venture between four different railway companies (LNWR/L&Y/GNR/NER), was amputated from the railway network after the last train had departed on Saturday 29 April 1967. Once the departure point of named expresses such as *The West Riding Pullman*, *The White Rose* and *The Queen of Scots Pullman* the 1-in-100 incline immediately outside the station, necessary to clear the Leeds and Liverpool Canal, was often the scene for spectacular starts – the locomotives slipping on wet/greasy rails with their heavy trains. The cramped seven-platformed (and two-bayed) above-street-level station of Leeds Central was, after nationalisation, always going to be a candidate for consolidation. It was an easy solution, albeit eight years from planning to implementation, with slewed pointwork at Whitehall Junction, a mere half mile outside the station, offering a new link enabling Doncaster and Kings Cross traffic to access Leeds City station. The site was cleared and acquired by the Post Office and all that remains to remind residents there today is the blue plaqued remnants of the erstwhile wagon hoist (used to raise/lower wagons between the low (road level) and high (rail level) goods yard) and, over the nearby canal, remains of the disused viaduct itself.

The disastrous side effect, from a steam chaser's view, of the closure was the cessation of the Wakefield Westgate/Bradford Exchange portions that had been routed via Wortley West Curve. This short connecting spur was subsequently lifted in 1985 notwithstanding vociferous concerns from Bradford residents fearing the presage, subsequently proving unfounded, of the end of through services to London. The portions, which were detached from the Kings Cross/Leeds Central services, had with few exceptions remained steam operated – the authorities never attempting to diagram diesels aware of their short-term future. Although Bradford Exchange bound passengers from London and the south could still travel on through services (albeit much reduced in numbers) by enduring a reversal at Leeds City these services predictably ceased in the early '70s. The other Bradford station at Forster Square became relegated to secondary status with only departures for Ilkley and Skipton – all previously portioned services for Leeds and the south ceasing forthwith. Taking all the above into consideration I made a concerted effort to travel on the doomed portions on all four Saturdays of that April leading up to the closure.

On the first of those April Saturdays, with Engelbert Humperdinck's *Release Me* topping the charts, as always the aperitif of the Calder Valley mail trains was imbibed upon arrival in the area. As with all visits accessing this mail train scenario, I had to depart from St Pancras the previous evening, changing at Sheffield, onto the now dieselised 02 00 departure, and Normanton. I sometimes, for the sheer hell of it, started out from London on an earlier than necessary train, changing at Kettering and Nottingham, purely (wait for it) to catch runs with several of the Peak diesel locomotives. No I wasn't changing into modern traction chasing, I had always noted every EL and DL that I travelled behind anyway – they were, after all, still numbers in Ian Allan's *Combined Volume* that could be redlined!

Returning to that first visit of '67, at Normanton one of Wakefield's two remaining Black 5s, 44990, took us the 22 miles from Normanton to Halifax on the 02 10 York/Manchester, handing over to Newton Heath's 45271. As always alighting at Hebden Bridge, a station awarded the accolade of the annual best kept station in 1965 by the NER management, at 05 05 after a mere twenty-three-minute wait the arrival of the 04 20 Manchester/York train produced on that particular morning Holbeck's 45075 – indeed on the few remaining occasions that summer I caught the eastbound train it was always a 55A locomotive. Not staying on the train beyond Normanton, perhaps it was either a DL on a non-required steam, we travelled over to Manchester, fingers crossed, for what had been seen in the LMR Special Traffic Notices as a possible steam-worked 'footex' (a train chartered for football supporters). Always monitoring the relevant region's STNs for any variations/reliefs/extras that offered possible steam haulage, we had spotted a 1X17 11 31 footex between Manchester and Leeds that day. Who was playing whom we didn't care, the subsequently preserved but then Patricroft-allocated Standard 5MT 73096 (noisily banked the 1¾ miles to Miles Platting by 44697) being turned out for the

43-mile journey over the Pennines. She wasn't in the best of health and having struggled with the eleven-coach train stopped for a two-minute 'blow up' at Diggle Junction — after which a 52½mph was maxed through Golcar.

While all the fans went to the match we filled in the five-hour turnaround with far more beneficial things than kicking a lump of air-filled spherical polyhedron around — we went portion bashing! We made our way to the recently opened station at New Pudsey — a relatively rare event in those days of the retrenchment-minded BR. The station's accompanying publicity flyer avowed 'incorporating sufficient car parking space to enable motorists from large residential areas north of Leeds and Bradford to use main line train services without having to negotiate congested city streets'. This additional station stop enabled greater flexibility for us enthusiasts with the ability to change on/off the portions — no intermediate stops being made prior to then. From there we caught Fairburn 2-6-4T 42235 the 3½ miles into Bradford Exchange.

In those pre-Internet/fast communication days the only method of keeping up to date with locomotive transfers and withdrawals was via magazines such as *The Railway World*, and even that, bearing in mind it was a monthly publication, reflected changes occurring retrospectively. Why am I highlighting this? Well we all had 42235 down as a Springs Branch (Wigan) locomotive! As if the day couldn't get any more special (an allusion to Frank & Nancy Sinatra's *Somethin' Stupid* riding high in the charts at the time), a mere forty-five minutes after arriving into Bradford the 15 05 departure had sister Fairburn 42287, transferred in from Trafford Park three months previously, taking us the 17 miles to Wakefield Westgate. I'd had six required haulages so far — could the luck continue? The answer, in the form of a lost-looking Lostock Hall-allocated 45226, was yes — she being turned out by Wakefield for the 16 28 portion into Bradford Exchange. Time was running out for the returning 18 15 footex departure from Leeds and so, having undertaken the short walk across to Bradford's Forster Square, a run with Manningham's Fairburn 42085 on the three-coach 17 27 Sheffield departure took us the 13½ miles via Shipley to Leeds City.

Although the returning footex departed only a few minutes late it was immediately obvious the fans were drowning their sorrows with wanton abandonment (it was a 6th Round FA Cup match — Leeds United 1 Manchester City 0). Despite having police presence on board, with their dogs, the communication cord was pulled on several occasions with fire extinguishers either being set off or thrown out of the window. We enthusiasts contained ourselves in several compartments — feet wedged firmly against the corridor doors to foil any attempted incursion by the marauding mob. We were more concerned about whether or not the connection with the 20 55 *Belfast Boat Express* departure was going to be made. We arrived into the Exchange station sixty-eight minutes late, at 20 50, giving us just five minutes to run the length of Europe's longest railway platform to the adjacent Victoria station — just making it with the welcoming sight of Carnforth's 45134 (my ninth requirement of the day!) impatient to get going.

This visit 'oop north' was top and tailed with SR steam outings on the Friday and Sunday and I was well and truly knackered upon arrival back home, having been out over sixty hours – but hey ho, with a steam mileage of 905 it made it all worthwhile. After reading one of my articles in the railway press a few years ago a long-term friend said, 'Your youth appears to have been spent in perpetual motion.' Having just reread this paragraph I am inclined to agree. Would I be as lucky the following week?

The short answer to that was no! With Britain celebrating Sandie Shaw's *Puppet on a String* win at the Eurovision Song Contest (no ex-Iron Curtain country block voting then!), Saturday 15 April saw some of us congregating at Carlisle at the unearthly hour of 01 30 tempted by the showing in the LMR STN of a 1X12 22 20 footex from Glasgow to Euston. Having previously ascertained it was to be Brit-worked, via Ais Gill to boot, our hopes, never taken for granted, were vindicated as Brit 70033 *Charles Dickens* came down from Kingmoor in readiness. Unfortunately an almost similar replication of last week's delays was to befall us, i.e. drunken 'fans', police and their dogs, not helped by a preceding parcels train catching fire at Blackburn – all contributing to an eventual 155-minute late arrival into Crewe. Upon arrival there, at 07 53, we were signalled into the non-platformed middle road. Not a problem for us enthusiasts and using our BR1 carriage key (all doors had been locked en route) we scrambled out, crossed a running line and clambered onto the platform. We had been spotted, not by the police but by the train's occupants and we quickly scarpered from the scene – glancing back to see a line of marauding fans following us out of the unlocked door!

Although all the above is not particularly relevant to this book I have included reference to the journey as a way of explaining my late arrival that Saturday into the NER. After that debacle I left Crewe, changing at Stockport, travelling over the line currently served by one parliamentarian train per week but back then offering prospective customers one per hour, for Stalybridge. Onwards over the Pennines and by changing once again, this time at Mirfield, an eventual arrival time of 10 44 was made into Wakefield Kirkgate.

Walking to the Westgate station I waited, and waited and waited – for something required to materialise. Services had first commenced running from this station precisely 100 years previously and was, at the time of my visit, undergoing a much needed renovation – the areas away from the platforms resembling something akin to a building site. Over the years Wakefield's Westgate station has seen a substantial increase in patronage, primarily resulting from the increased frequency of services consequential from the electrification of the line in 1989. So much so that a re-sited station, as part of the Westgate Key Development Area, was formally opened in February 2014 by the Secretary of State Patrick McLoughlin MP – the former 'no longer fit for purpose'. After a three-hour wait the solitary run I had on that April '67 day in the area was with Low Moor-allocated Fairburn 42055 on the 13 42 portion to Bradford. This Fairburn, having spent the first thirteen years of her life working suburban services out of Glasgow Central, was, to put it bluntly, becoming painfully common. After last week's highs this was a definite low.

The success or failure, in a chaser's eyes, was always dictated by the number of required catches and, without any other possibilities circulating that day, I cut my losses, returning to Carlisle for another Brit – on the soon to be dieselised last surviving booked steam crossing over the border: the 20 32 Carlisle to Perth. The weekend, however, was far from finished. Upon returning to Euston on the Sunday morning I boarded The Mercian rail tour (detailed in Chapter 11), which, courtesy of preserved locomotives 3442 *The Great Marquess* and 4472 *Flying Scotsman*, took me on a circular trip from Euston via Bolton, Keighley and Leeds Central to Kings Cross.

So to the third Saturday – 22 April. Had I exhausted all that was available? Expecting the worst, the ritual of the Calder Valley mail services was once more partaken of, reaping a surprising catch of Stockport's 44836 on the Low Moor's Normanton departure at 03 10 (locomotives allocated to depots with no booked passenger duties were eagerly welcomed because of their rarity value).

Taken over at Halifax with the extremely common Newton Heath 44891, I was less than delighted with Holbeck's 45211, a locomotive caught working a Nottingham/Marylebone train ten months previous, turning up at Hebden Bridge on the eastbound Manchester/York. With no passenger work allocated to the class anywhere in Britain I was more than made up upon arrival into Normanton, where the Manchester locomotive was taken off and the foreman sent out his home depot's LMS Mogul 43043.

Not always bothering (other than on the Southern) to take accurate passing times/speeds with my ever-present stopwatch, it seems, judging from my tattered notebook, this day was an exception – with all trains caught that day onwards being recorded thus. With her 3c/1v load, the 'Flying Pig' was easily able to maintain time through the low-lying farmland – a max of 60mph passing Burton Salmon leading to a two-minute early arrival into York.

Travelling over to Leeds I reaped a run with a Type 2 'Splutterbug' (D5237) on a Forster Square portion before crossing to the Exchange for another run with Low Moor's Fairburn 42116 on the 11 00 portion for Leeds Central – maxing at, with her 4c load, 50mph passing through Bramley. Heading south to Wakefield for the 13 42 Bradford portion (third week in a row on this train!) what should follow me there but 42116. This time, however, she was a little livelier (perhaps with only a 3c load) attaining 58mph north of Beeston Junction before slamming the brakes on for the speed-restricted Wortley Curves.

Ex-Trafford Park, now Wakefield-allocated 42574, one of only a handful of Stanier 2-6-4Ts remaining, returned me to Wakefield, twice obtaining 62mph during the thirty-six-minute, 17-mile three-vehicle train. Last year, having spent the day chasing in the area, there was always the one-coach 22 00 Bradford/Huddersfield to return home on (via Wigan!), but, since it was now missing from the timetable (public anyway),

Extracts from notebook.

21st April 1967					
via Wimbledon			7½	S+3/11	
17 09	Waterloo	1L	34013	47¾	
18 28	Basingstoke	3L	—	—	
19 34	Basingstoke	2E	34102	47¾	
20 16	Waterloo	04E	—	—	
21 30	St Pancras	✓	D50	158½	
01 03	Sheffield Mid.	1AL	—	—	
22nd April	—	—	—	—	
02 00	Sheffield Mid	✓	D119	28½	
02 32	Normanton	3L	—	■	
03 10	Normanton	1L	44836*	22	
↓	Halifax	—	44391	8¾	
05 05	Hebden Bridge	✓	—	·	
05 22	Hebden Bridge	6L	45211	27¼	
↓	Normanton	—	43093*	24½	
07 50	York	2G	—	—	
07 57	York	2L	NR	24½	
08 32	Normanton	2E	—	—	Y0025 cm
08 41	Normanton	✓	D22 *	11	55.7
↓	Leeds City	—	D5237*	135	
09 43	Bradford F.S	14L	—	·	
11 00	Bradford Exchange	1L	42116	9½	
11 20	Leeds Central	2L	—	·	
12 42	Leeds Central	✓	NR	10	
13 00	Wakefield Westgate	✓	—	·	
13 42	Wakefield Westgate	12L	42116	18	
14 22	Bradford Exchange	13L	—	—	

15 05	Bradford Exchange	1L	42574	18
15 41	Wakefield Westgate	4E	—	—
16 28	Wakefield Westgate	✓	44826*	18
17 05	Bradford Exchange	✓	—	—
17 20	Bradford Exchange	1L	42233*	9½
↓	Leeds Central		09012 *	125¾
21 02	Kings Cross	✓	—	·
via LB/PW				11

No More Wakefield Portions

Extracts from notebook.

I was inclined to call it a day at 16 00 – unless otherwise persuaded. Suitable persuasion, in the form of a required Holbeck 44826, turned up from Wakefield shed for the 16 28 Bradford portion. After 44826 deposited me at Bradford Exchange I had already decided to catch the 17 20 all the way to Kings Cross. I couldn't have been more pleased, a grin from ear to ear perhaps surprising some normal customers, on sighting the motive power for it. Ex-Springs Branch (Wigan), now Low Moor, Fairburn 42233 (subsequently withdrawn five days later) worked the 9½ miles to Leeds Central, driver Johnson maxing at 53mph through Bramley – Deltic D9012 *Crepello* taking me forward to Kings Cross at 21 02 that night. A rare Saturday night in my own bed!

During those far-off dying days of the Iron Horse you couldn't be everywhere at the same time. Train services were being dieselised, lines were closing and the last remaining examples of many classes of steam locomotive were sometimes specifically steamed up for final occasions. The final weekend of Leeds Central was another example – it clashing with the withdrawal of Scotland's steam allocation (in reality many more incursions were made into Scotland throughout the summer of '67 – but were with English-allocated power). How did we solve this one? The answer lay in taking a valuable annual leave day on Friday 28 April – not particularly perturbed by that day's news that the UK applied for EEC membership. By doing this Jock (it had to be him didn't it!) and I caught the few remaining suburban steam services out of Glasgow on the Friday morning, bashing Motherwell, Corkerhill and Polmadie sheds during the day, before heading south to Carlisle for the Brit-worked 20 32 Perth departure.

Backtracking to Carlisle we tried to get some shut-eye while travelling over Ais Gill in the early hours of Saturday 29 April en route to Leeds. Arriving into the City station at just gone 3 a.m. the short walk between there and the Central station held no fears – even though all previous occasions had been during daylight hours. Indeed I had often crossed between termini within major cities, e.g. Liverpool, Manchester, Sheffield and London, in the dead of night. In the case of London, although if you had the patience to wait there were eventually buses or tubes, arriving on Sunday mornings into either Marylebone at 05 06 (22 50 ex-Manchester) or Euston at 02 40 (20 46 ex-Barrow) I usually walked across London. Perhaps it was the naivety of youth that saw me avoid any 'problems' such as one could encounter today. Unlike today's twenty-four-hour binge-drinking climate with its associated antisocial disorder, back then, with the licensed outlets having all closed by midnight, the streets, the odd vagrant excepted, were deserted. Occasional approaches by ladies of the night enquiring if I wanted 'to spend a little time with them' being responded to by pleading poverty.

Not many West Riding-allocated tanks escaped me but this one did. Transferred in from Trafford Park in November 1966, Fairburn 42267 is seen at Halifax on 8 April 1967 having arrived with a lightweight parcels service. This 20-year-old Wakefield locomotive was withdrawn the following month.

An unknown location sees a collection of like-minded friends from all over Britain – it was obviously a cold morning and, guessing by the fatigued expressions, almost certainly after an overnight bash. The author being 5th from the left.

One of 55E's two Fairburns, life-long resident 42149, at Normanton on 22 April 1967. Although being withdrawn three months hence I had fortunately caught her into York the previous October.

About to be detached from the 04 25 Manchester Victoria to York, the Newton Heath foreman had returned Holbeck's 4-6-0 45211 back to the NER on 22 April 1967. She was withdrawn a mere three weeks later aged 32.

What a winner this catch was! Anything could be turned out by the Normanton foreman to take the 04 25 ex-Manchester forward to York. On 22 April 1967 55E's Flying Pig Ivatt 4MT 43043 was supplied – this Horwich-built Mogul surviving until the October cull. This was one of two remaining booked steam passenger services into York (the other being the 17 47 FO ex-Manchester) and was to be dieselised within weeks.

Holbeck's 44852 is at the helm of the 10 05 *Devonian* out of Bradford Forster Square on 22 April 1967. This Crewe-built 33-year-old was to work this Paignton-bound departure the 13½ miles to Leeds City. The extensive sidings in the background are where the present relocated station has been built.

With withdrawal just two months away Low Moor's 2-6-4T 42116 awaits the off at Bradford Exchange with the 11 00 portion for Wakefield Westgate on 22 April 1967, en route to Kings Cross. She, together with sister 42184, had monopolised the afternoon Stockport departure the previous year.

Leeds Central station had just eight days remaining before closure – services being concentrated on the adjacent Leeds City. Holbeck-allocated Fairburn 42699 awaits her next duties on 22 April 1967 – her own demise coming in seventeen days' time.

Anyway, rant over, back to Leeds and having undertaken the short walk to the Central station we found Newton Heath's 44846 at the head of the 03 32 departure for Halifax. Travelling via the then freight-only spur between Laisterdyke and Bowling Junction this four-coach set, upon arrival at Halifax, formed the somewhat circuitously routed 08 48 portion to Wakefield Westgate via Huddersfield. I also believe the 03 32 upon which we travelled was the last (I am prepared to be corrected – any amendment can be put through at reprint) booked steam working out of Leeds Central, the station closing after the final departure, a DMU for Harrogate, that evening. The Black 5 duly took over the 02 10 York at Halifax and after alighting at Hebden Bridge the welcome sight of Holbeck's 45219 hove into view with the eastbound York train. I wasn't to catch any other required locomotive that day.

After arrival into Normanton, with nothing worth travelling with on its forward journey to York, we headed south to Cudworth to pick up the 07 06 Sheffield Midland to Leeds City, which turned up with Holbeck's 45075. A newly delivered D7570 took us over to Bradford Forster Square in order to catch the 10 00 *The Devonian* departure with another 55A Blackie, 44826. *My* last departure out of Leeds Central (albeit with D1764) took us to Wakefield Westgate where, after catching 44826 again on the 12 24 portion as far as New Pudsey, we changed onto Fairburn 42196 on the 14 19 arrival into Bradford Exchange. This was the fourth Saturday on the trot travelling on this portion and, with nothing in circulation that I hadn't already had a run with, I called it a day and set off on a 105-mile DMU journey over Ais Gill to Carlisle for another ride with a Brit into Scotland. Upon returning to London, did I go straight home? Not a chance: a further 216 return steam miles to Bournemouth were enjoyed before wending my way home after another sixty-hour bash.

So summing up those four weeks, although catching recent tank transfers in from the LMR, there was, in comparison with last year, a noticeable absence of the LNER B1s – three of which, subsequent research has revealed, were still on Wakefield's books. And I was disappointed with the increased proliferation of Type 2 diesels on the Forster Square portions – there were still some Holbeck Black 5s and tanks I would like to have caught. You can't win them all! Two weeks later, on 5 May, Yorkshire's first motorway link to London, the M1, was completed – further eroding the falling passenger numbers using rail.

Holbeck-allocated Black 5 44826 calls at the recently opened New Pudsey station, 3½ miles out of Bradford, on 29 April 1967 with the 12 24 portion from Wakefield Westgate to Bradford Exchange.

A second view of Stanier 5MT 44826 at New Pudsey – this Crewe-built 33-year-old surviving until the October cull that year.

After an hour's wait from the previous shot, Low Moor's 42196 arrives at New Pudsey on 29 April 1967 with the portion off the 10 20 Kings Cross to Leeds Central. Leeds Central station closed later that day and from the following Monday the few remaining Kings Cross/Bradford through services were routed via Leeds City.

14

THE WEST RIDING FINALE

DURING THAT SUMMER of '67 steam sheds were closing akin to a pile of dominoes – Manningham in April, Wakefield in June with York becoming diesel only the same month. By July just three – Holbeck, Low Moor and Normanton – remained, the four others in the coalfields of Durham and East Midlands not having passenger work. With Leeds Central having been closed in the April of 1967, resulting in the cessation of the steam-operated portions, there was little to entice haulage bashers such as myself to the area. One of the few remaining trains where steam power could be guaranteed was the Calder Valley-routed 02 10 York/Manchester mails service, which during that June I often used as a means to access the still steam-saturated LMR.

From the following month, after the cessation of steam on the SR, a notable increase in 'clientele' from the south helped swell the numbers participating in this nightly charade to worryingly overcrowded proportions. On one occasion (22 July) information as to the locomotive that was to take over at Halifax (upon reversal) coupled with a not-required tank on it at Normanton led me to abandon any attempt at obtaining even standing space on the westbound train. I headed south to Sheffield that morning and, having endured a two-hour fester at the Midland station, I travelled out on what had become the sole remaining steam departure from the city – the 07 06 for Leeds (45428). It was all coming to an end. With the NER steam cull at the end of September all that was to remain was Newton Heath's provision of Black 5s for the 03 32 Leeds/Halifax and Manchester on the westbound service and from Manchester to Normanton on the eastbound – the latter (already reduced to steam operation MO) going diesel weeks later. In just twelve months the six-locomotive circuit had changed to one.

After the cessation of the WCML summer Saturday-dated services that year several non-railway activities, including an office weekend outing to Jersey, resulted in a hiatus of steam chasing. I felt, however, out of sheer nostalgic respect for the area that one final visit had to be made. By now the allocation of steam within the NER had diminished to a mere 124 – the LNER examples including just four Q6, seven J27 and three B1s – only the latter, all subsequently reallocated to Low Moor, surviving beyond the beginning of September.

So now to the last weekend of steam passenger trains in Yorkshire. On Friday 29 September, an evening when the inaugural episode of the cult *The Prisoner*, starring Patrick McGoohan, was aired I travelled from Kings Cross to York to connect with the last steam-worked (from Normanton) 02 10 York/Manchester. Topping the charts then, somewhat prophetically, was Engelbert Humperdinck's *The Last Waltz*. I had selected this route rather than run the risk of a missed connection at Normanton out of the 02 00 ex-Sheffield. An hour's mooch around a now steamless York was endured before the stock for the 02 10 departure for Manchester was platformed, at the head of which, filling the air with her obnoxious fumes, was 'Long Pong' D258. I can't remember there being many, if any, enthusiasts on board – the situation changing dramatically upon arrival into Normanton with the expected invasion of chasers materialising. What steam, on this final night, was to take forward to Halifax? LMS 2-6-4T 42689, a locomotive I had never witnessed in my travels, was the answer. Where had she been hiding? Research for this book revealed this ex-Scottish Fairburn had, upon arrival in the NER, been allocated to Leeds Neville Hill before spending time at Huddersfield and Royston, arriving at Holbeck in April '67 and finally being transferred to Low Moor in her final month. That was a good start to the visit, only to be further improved with a required Edge Hill 45287 taking over at Halifax.

So Hebden Bridge was alighted at for the last time – a seemingly regular 'Splutterbug' (D7572) on the eastbound for York taking me back to Normanton. With nothing noted in my book as to what took over there, I can only presume it to be another DL. I headed the 10 miles south to Cudworth, boarding the very last steam train out of Sheffield, the 0706 for Leeds City, with a lost looking Lostock Hall 44971 in charge. It had been hoped, at least among the enthusiast fraternity, that the two remaining Jubilees, *Alberta* and *Kolhapur*, might have been turned out. Perhaps the authorities, similar to the SR finale debacle the previous July, didn't want to draw attention to themselves in having taken this length of time to eliminate steam.

```
Friday 29th September 1967
                    VIA WIMBLEDON                    7        +3/6
   E 6024 ] Waterloo - Basingstoke         47½      23/-
   E 6027 ]
        [ 1730 Waterloo to Bournemouth ]
   D 1925     Basingstoke - Woking         23½
        [ 1550 Weymouth Quay to Waterloo ]
   EMU        Woking - Waterloo            24¼
        [ 1730 Portsmouth & Sea to Waterloo ]

2020  | Kings Cross        | 2L | D9003     | 188
Saturday 30th September 1967
0009  | York               | ✓  | —         | —
0210  | - York             | 3L | D258      | 24½
  ↓   | Normanton          |    | 42689     | 22
      | Holyar             |    | 45237     | 8
0505  | Hebden Bridge      | 16L| —         | —
0528  | Hebden Bridge      | 2L | D7572     | 27½
0650  | Normanton          | 10L| —         | —
0712  | Normanton          | ✓  | D142      | 10     A2251 0912
0737  | Cudworth           | ✓  | —         | —      Balt- BP
0752  | Cudworth           | 2L | 44371     | 21
0851  | Leeds City         | 9L | —         | —
0905  | Leeds City         | 2L | NR        | 9½
0926  | Bradford Exchange  | 3L | —         | —      'YORKSHIRE
0955  | Bradford Exchange  | ✓  | 61306     | 9½      PULLMAN'
1017  | Leeds City         | 7L | —         | —
1130  | Leeds City         | ✓  | D1582     | 10
1448  | Wakefield Westgate | ✓  | —         | —
```

Extracts from my notebook.

```
1208  Wakefield Westgate   ✓  *D26    10   45562 } 5SA    61306/3 Pull Iron/ —      45428/3c/ —
1223  Leeds City           ✓   —      —    45593                              1420 Leeds City
1235  Leeds City           ✓  *D165   10   45697         0955 Bradford Ex.   L  0000
1254  Wakefield Westgate   ✓   —      —    chiney man     B  0000             WJ 0157  28
1334  Wakefield Westgate   5L  D173   10   44912 } 33A   StD 0244  115/7      H  0238  26
1354  Leeds City           5L  —      —    44902          H  0624  14½      WW 0408   28
1420  Leeds City           ✓   45428  9½   #7029 on      L  0911  17/41½     A  0538   29½
1446  Bradford Exchange    ✓   —      —    Railtour      NP 1223              B  0827   46½
1505  Bradford Exchange    ✓   D7570  9½                 S  0136  39         S  0956   44
  ↓   Leeds City           ✓   D1105  10                 B  0258  5½         NP 1115
1553  Wakefield Westgate   ✓  *D1509  10                 A  0529  41/20     L  0337   15
1620  Wakefield Westgate   ✓   45428  6                  WW 0657  22½       H  0505   40
  ↓   Leeds City           ✓   —      —                  sigs { 0836          sigs { 06 23
1708  New Pudsey           ✓   —      —                       { 0804                { 0648
1731  New Pudsey           1L  D390   6                  H  0901  16        StD 0720  13½
1742  Leeds City           4L  —      —                  sigs { 0936         B  0943
1747  Leeds City           2L *D1109  43                      { 1226
1905  Manchester Exchange  2E  —      —                  WJ 1321  10
1940  Manchester Victoria  3L  NR     30½                LCJ 1413  5
2027  Preston              ✓   —      —                  L  1939
2125  Preston              8L  45421  28½  45238 on 204R
2203  Liverpool Exchange   10L —      —    45187 on 1010U
2250  Liverpool Lime Street 5L NR     31
J005  Manchester Exchange  3L  —      —
Sunday 1st October                                       0255  Wigan North Western   ? D1960  38½
0100  Manchester Exchange  —   45136  17½                  ↓   Crewe                 ? E3423 158
0136  Wigan NW             3L  —      —                   ?   Euston
                                                              via BF/3AY              15½
```

On 30 September 1967 a lost-looking Lostock Hall-allocated 5MT 44971 drifts into Cudworth with the very last steam train out of Sheffield – the 07 06 Sheffield Midland to Leeds City. She was more fortunate than all her NER-allocated cousins, not being withdrawn until the very end of BR steam the following August.

The very last occasion I travelled over the London extension of the ex-Great Central was on 23 August 1966. Here, at Marylebone, was Hull Dairycoates-allocated 4-6-0 B1 61306 having worked in on the 08 15 ex-Nottingham Victoria, and should have returned on the train I was about to board, the 14 38. She was, however, failed with hot bearings and although disappointed in its replacement, being a 'Splutterbug' (Class 25), matters improved when a BR 9F freight locomotive was turned out for the 16 38. Little did I know I was to eventually have a run with her thirteen months later (see next shot).

Bradford Low Moor shed was recoded in its final month from 56F to 55J – B1 4-6-0 61306 proudly displaying her newly acquired smokebox shed code. This 19-year-old North British-built B1 was one of three transferred into Low Moor three months earlier upon the closure to steam of Hull Dairycoates. Bulled up, no doubt by MNA members, for the final steam-working *Yorkshire Pullman* for London Kings Cross she is seen on 30 September 1967 prior to the 09 55 departure from Bradford Exchange. To partake a run with her the 9½ miles to Leeds we, and there were plenty of 'anoraks', willingly forked out a 3/6d supplement. Although she was withdrawn upon closure of Low Moor the following day she is one of two surviving B1s to be preserved and is currently based at the North Norfolk Railway. This was my last day's visit to what had become my favourite station in the region, Bradford Exchange. Why favourite? Well being a relatively small terminus it epitomised the steam era, oozing atmosphere. Anything could be caught from there – tanks, B1s, Jubilees and Black 5s – just wonderful!

We enthusiasts expected at least one of the remaining Jubilees to be turned out for the final weekend of steam in the West Riding, but excepting the B1 out of Bradford earlier that morning the only other steam working was this. At least Holbeck bulled up their pet Black 5, the now-preserved 45428 seen here at Leeds City on 30 September 1967 with the 14 20 departure for Bradford Exchange.

The West Riding Finale

The 'intruder' in Yorkshire on 30 September 1967 was the privately preserved GWR 4-6-0 7029 *Clun Castle*, which took over a London/Carlisle rail tour at Peterborough. Here she is, ten months earlier, performing similar duties at Stourbridge Junction.

With nothing happening at Leeds we went over to Bradford for what, retrospectively, was to be the highlight of the day. The Low Moor foreman sent out one of his three recently acquired B1s, 61306, for the 09 55 departure out of Bradford Exchange. The locomotive had been externally cleaned overnight by members of the MNA organisation and was a credit to their hard work. This was Britain's final steam-operated prestige train *The Yorkshire Pullman* – the white-coated silver-service car attendants making an unexpected cash haul with all us enthusiasts having, not begrudgingly mind, to pay the necessary 3s 6d (32½p) supplement. A disappointing signal-delayed 9½-mile run over to Leeds City was undertaken with a max of a mere 54½mph near Bramley giving us a seven-minute late arrival into Leeds – the starter course of soup not being served until all us degenerates had alighted there! With nothing much going on during the remainder of the morning a couple of fill-in trips to/from Wakefield (sad wasn't I?) reaped runs with three Peaks and one Brush 4 noting, when passing Holbeck, Black 5 44902 (12A) and the two 'missing' miscreant Jubilees in light steam, 45697 *Achilles* (chimney missing) and 44912 being in the withdrawn line.

A Great Western intruder, in the form of privately owned 4-6-0 7029 *Clun Castle*, was also evident in the area while working a rail tour. Holbeck's 45428, scrubbed up for the occasion, was turned out for the 14 20 Leeds City to Bradford Exchange, returning light engine to work the 13 25 Kings Cross/Bradford Exchange forward ex-Leeds City at 16 50. Darkness was now falling and, considering the day a bit of a damp squib,

I cut my losses and went over to Preston for the evening's portions – trains that were to enter railway folklore history by becoming Britain's last steam-hauled public services.

That was it then as regards the NER's passenger workings. The few steam movements the next day (as read about afterwards) culminated in Low Moor's 42152 working the final portion, the 16 18 departure out of Bradford Exchange. The following Monday saw Low Moor shed completely close, Holbeck and Normanton losing their steam allocations but retaining servicing facilities for visiting LMR locomotives.

So how did I fare as regards the catches during my forty-two visits during the final eighteen months of steam in the North Eastern Region? I accrued runs with 119 different locomotives from twelve different classes – with the obvious dominance of Stanier's Black 5s. The Exchange portions in particular provided a wonderful selection of motive power, among which many Thompson B1s and Stanier/Fairburn tanks were often chanced across. Then there was the initial attraction of the nine Jubilees – without which perhaps the number of visits might well have been fewer. With both Bradford and Leeds stations having been exited/arrived into on just over thirty occasions behind steam, only Leeds City remains today anything vaguely familiar from those wonderful days (and nights!) of yesteryear.

In a résumé of the statistics shown in Appendix 11; in April 1966 there were eighty-one steam locomotives available at six depots available (on paper at least!) for passenger traffic. By that October, taking into account withdrawals and transfers in, seventy remained – of which I'd caught runs with thirty-eight (54 per cent). Not visiting the area during that winter the numbers had fallen, by April 1967, to fifty-six – with my captures reduced to twenty-eight (50 per cent). The withdrawal of Bradford portions and the closure of Manningham and Wakefield sheds further reduced numbers to forty-one by the August of '67 – of which thirty-one (75 per cent) had fallen into my clutches. There were, excluding Royston's 8Fs, a mere thirty-one steam locomotives (on paper) remaining at the end; made up of eleven Fairburn/one Stanier tanks, fourteen Black 5s, two Jubilees and three B1s shared between Holbeck, Normanton and Low Moor, of which I required just five – not bad for someone living over 200 miles distant. These withdrawals meant that the Fairburn/Stanier tanks together with the B1 classes of steam locomotives became extinct. The final duty for an NER-allocated steam locomotive was enacted on 4 November 1967 – with Royston's 48276.

15

AND STILL THEY COME

PERHAPS THE NER authorities had hoped, after the October 1967 cull of their own allocation, that they, or more pertinently the foremen at their sheds, would have no further dealings with steam. They hadn't, however, contemplated the still steam-infested neighbouring region of the LMR forwarding many specials, both freight and passenger, over the 'border'. In addition to those there were two services that remained diagrammed for steam until the end of '67. The first of these was the 17 37 (FO) Manchester Exchange to York whose calling points were at Stalybridge (17 55), Huddersfield (18 25) and Leeds City (18 55) prior to arrival into York at 19 34. This was part of a Kingmoor Britannia duty and, taking into consideration to travel on it would cost me a day's annual leave, it wasn't until June 1967 when, as was often the case, although booked for a Kingmoor Brit, a 12A Black 5 (44911) was the power. Departing from the Exchange station, this lengthy train was always assisted in the rear up Miles Platting bank, the sight and sound of two steam locomotives being opened up in anticipation of the assault of the climb, no doubt startling unsuspecting commuters waiting on the adjacent Victoria station as they stormed past.

From June 1967 the train started at 17 47 and was diverted via the Calder Valley route and on 4 August another 12A Black 5 (44817 – withdrawn eight days later) took me to Leeds. I returned to LMR metals on that occasion via Diggle on a Manchester/Holyhead service starting back at Leeds with Holbeck-allocated 45219. Steam each way over the Pennines as late as August '67 was a notable event. It wasn't until my fourth and final trip on the train that I actually had a run with the booked power, Brit 70051 *Firth of Forth* on Friday 3 November, travelling the entire 76 miles through to York. Having accumulated nearly 7,000 miles with a total of thirty-nine members of the Britannia class over a mere twenty-six months, this was to be my last run with one on a public service train. The locomotive off this Friday working was often returned to the LMR each Monday via the 03 32 Leeds/Halifax/Manchester and with Kingmoor's closure to steam on 31 December (70013 *Oliver Cromwell* working the final 17 47 departure on Friday 29 December) the train went DL. Kingmoor had, up until its closure, continued to send Brits, LMS 8Fs and Black 5s over the

Only possible because of a Christmas present of a flash attachment for my camera, Newton Heath's Black 5 45310 waits at Leeds City on a bitterly cold February morning in 1968 with the 03 32 departure for Halifax. This particular locomotive annoyingly (from a chaser's point of view) worked this train on many occasions during those final months of penetration by LMR-allocated locomotives into the diesel desert the NER had become. She even survived the shed's closure that July, being withdrawn at Carnforth just a week prior to the end that August.

Long Drag on freights right through that autumn and there were several instances of Christmas passenger specials worked by LMR Manchester area-allocated steam locomotives over to Leeds, but I wasn't privy, or in the area, to sample them.

The second booked incursion into the NER was the 23 38 (SuO) Liverpool Lime Street/York – worked by a Patricroft Standard 5MT as far as Leeds. This called at Manchester Victoria (00 33), Huddersfield (01 20) arriving into Leeds at 01 50 and combining there with the 21 53 ex-Shrewsbury for York (03 11). This was an awkward train to cover with work on the Monday morning at my desk job at Wimbledon, but enticed by the desire to travel on one of the country's longest steam-hauled passenger journeys remaining (74 miles) I managed it on seven occasions! My first visit was on the last Sunday of August '67 with 73073. It was a bank holiday that weekend and, with no need to attend work on the Monday, after arriving into Leeds at 01 50 I wandered across to the stock for the 03 32 Halifax departure, jumped in, fell asleep and woke upon the jerking departure – assured, by the noise from the front and the 'wet' steam heating in the compartment, that I hadn't boarded the wrong train. At Halifax, having found out that she was a required Kingmoor Black 5, I alighted and awaited the arrival of the 02 10 York/Manchester – the train 44775 was to take forward after berthing the Leeds stock away in the sidings. The Manchester train duly arrived and, making a beeline for an empty compartment, resumed my sleep quota that night on the one-and-a half-hour journey into Manchester.

Having thoroughly enjoyed the journey through the night on the Liverpool train I made plans to blitz the train on four consecutive Sundays that October. The first and third (73136/31) saw me alighting at Manchester Victoria at 00 30, then walking to the Exchange station for the 01 00 sleepers to Wigan en route to the office. On the second visit (73053) I stayed aboard at Manchester because, ever the track basher, the train was diverted, resulting from engineering work, under the wires at Guide Bridge and via the Stalybridge avoiding line. Travelling over rare freight routes such as this with steam was a novelty and being unaware of the revised arrival time into Leeds I was becoming concerned (about my London connection) until the lights of Leeds came into view at just gone 2 a.m. Although there were two southbound overnight services into St Pancras, at 02 23 and 03 15, the latter would not only have made me late into the office but more importantly I wouldn't have had time for the obligatory fry-up breakfast at the transport café in Eversholt Street, Euston prior to starting work. I needn't have worried – eventually making a leisurely thirteen-minute connection into the former – the 21 25 ex-Glasgow.

I hadn't planned on going through to Yorkshire any more occasions on that train, but on Bonfire Night (it was only that night back then – not the protracted week-long affair of these days!) that year upon arrival at Patricroft 73128 was exchanged, after an hour's delay, for 73132 – the former suffering a burnt-out ash pan. Although seeing Brit 70021 *Morning Star* on the 01 00 sleeper departure at Manchester Exchange when passing, as there was insufficient time to 'walk the walk' between the two stations I had no alternative but to stay aboard.

Unable to monitor the train's progress in the dark although fully appreciating the sterling efforts made by the crew I was fighting sleep deprivation in a bid not to miss the Leeds stop – every signal stop adding to my distress. She eventually arrived into Leeds at 02 59 (sixty-nine minutes late) that morning, forcing me to board the 03 15 (21 55 ex-Edinburgh) train into St Pancras. Being a slower (via Nottingham) service, after arriving into London at 08 16, forfeiting any breakfast and battling across in the rush hour, a tired and hungry enthusiast eventually arrived at his desk at 09 15 – nearly forty-five minutes late. I had not originally planned to stay out three nights that weekend, but having decided at the last minute to travel with *Oliver Cromwell* over Ais Gill on the Carlisle Kingmoor Rail Tour on the Sunday I arrived at the office that Monday morning with several days growth on my face and somewhat fragrant clothing! After commenting that 'I'd thought you'd have grown out of this sort of thing' (referring to the end of Southern steam earlier that year), my manager tactfully suggested that I took half a day's leave and go home – to which I acquiesced. At least I wasn't the two hours late that occurred in January '69 when having to explain to my manager (albeit a different one!) that, being aboard the last train over the Waverley route, I was delayed by a protest group blocking the railway with a tractor – the MP David Steele participating in the events.

With the Prime Minister Harold Wilson endorsing the 'I'm backing Britain' campaign, attempting to encourage workers to work extra hours without pay, Sunday 14 January 1968 saw me once more heading north for an attempt at catching runs on some of the ever-decreasing number of steam-operated passenger services. After savouring a required Black 5 on a Preston to Liverpool Exchange portion I had to fester for some hours on the cold windswept Liverpool Lime Street station and wasn't best pleased when espying a 'diseasel' (word coined by Thomas the Tank!) at the front of the 23 38 departure. Sitting with his feet on the console reading his paper in a warm cab environment I am sure the driver of Type 2 D5226 considered this a better option than a dirty run-down open-cabbed steam locomotive – an opinion rather selfishly not agreed with by myself.

The one final remaining steam penetration into the former NER therefore became the 03 32 Leeds/02 10 York/Manchester service. Officially the last NER shed to close to steam was Normanton in January 1968 and I therefore can only assume Holbeck still retained watering facilities, adequate coal being brought with her, for the 03 32 locomotive. Surprisingly remaining steam operated (Mondays excepted – MX) right through until the May, I used it on five occasions (one of which was another pesky Type 2 – the booked Black 5 having been declared a failure) during those final sad days of that last winter/spring. Louis Armstrong's *What a Wonderful World* was not exactly top of *my* charts. It was a warmer sleep-inducing method of accessing one of the few remaining steam services, that of the 09 00 Liverpool Exchange departure, than the alternative lengthy wait in the wooden-benched Wigan waiting room. The last reported booked working of the train by steam was on 11 May 1968 with 45310 – she, however, was failed and was replaced by a DL. Statistically I travelled on this service a stamina-busting twenty-six occasions – seriously contributing to the number of Stanier workhorses being caught. That fact in itself quantified why (at least to me) I still suffered thousands of electric and diesel miles to collect just a few with steam.

And finally, my last steam visit to the North Eastern Region on both regular passenger services and rail tours was on Saturday 27 April 1968, as follows:

Preservation Special No. 2 – Saturday 27 April 1968

LMS Stanier 5MT 4-6-0s 44781 and 45046 Stockport Edgeley (dep. 10 37) to Stalybridge via Peak Forest Junction and Guide Bridge = 46½ miles.
BR Standard 5MT 4-6-0s 73050 and 73069 Stalybridge to Bolton via Diggle, Huddersfield, Copy Pit and Darwin = 72¼ miles.
LMS 8F 2-8-0 48652 Bolton to Stockport Edgeley via Rochdale and Oldham = 32 miles.
BR 9F 2-10-0 92218 Stockport Edgeley to Liverpool Lime Street (arr. 18 31) via Northenden and Warrington Bank Quay = 36½ miles.

This jointly organised tour (Severn Valley Railway Society/Manchester Rail Travel Society) started and finished at Birmingham New Street. Having, the previous Saturday, come across two dolled up Black 5s at Stockport while mooching around the Manchester area, I attempted to board the rail tour they were about to work. On this occasion my usual 'board whatever steam train was running' powers deserted me. For whatever reason, either the ever alert organisers or unavailability of seats, I was thwarted, but luckily, owing to the heavy demand a repeat tour was scheduled for the following Saturday. A week later, and having travelled out of Manchester on Friday's Belfast Boat Express (BBE) with Carnforth 45025, I then went across to Yorkshire for my final steam departure out of Leeds (with the annoyingly common 45310) onto the 02 10 York/Manchester at Halifax.

With four hours to fill at Manchester before the tour I chanced a trip to Preston for that morning's BBE, expecting 45025 again but gratifyingly collecting a run with a required 10A 45394. This day's tour was the only occasion I'd had Standard 5s on NER metals and out of all the locomotives used only the subsequently preserved 73050 was dud. It was also the very last occasion a 9F was used on a passenger train. I had already booked the following Monday off and although I was prepared to stay up North the three nights with little on offer (i.e. that evening's Preston portions) a very contented gricer made his way south for a rare Saturday night in his own bed.

It was during those final dispiriting months when realising my hobby, to which I had dedicated all my leisure time over the previous few years, was being taken away from me that Bill, the original inspirational friend back in 1963, once again came to my rescue.

He highlighted the fact that there was plenty of steam available abroad and, depressed by the ever decreasing availability throughout Britain, I joined him on many European adventures (depicted in my first tome – *The Great Iron Horse Chase: Europe*).

The Love Affair's *Everlasting Love* was blasting the airwaves and for once reflected the reigniting of my own enthusiasm with one of man's greatest achievements. Later in '68 Mary Hopkins had a top-ten success with her *Those Were the Days*. The frantic search for the dying steam locomotive in their ever diminishing habitats to the accompaniment of the vibrant raw '60s music scene certainly, in my life, made that era unforgettable. While looking through my notebooks during research for this book I did wonder as to my mentality in spending hundreds of nights away from any warm comfortable bed. With steam seemingly becoming more and more confined to nocturnal services, where did the stamina and energy come from? I did it because I reasoned that it was all to end soon and I was witnessing history being made. I can honestly say that my hobby took me to many places I have never been to before (or again) all over Britain. I have met people, some of them with unfathomable dialects, from all walks of life in situations, locations and environments never imagined. I am that much wiser for the wonderful experience my hobby has given me and I wouldn't have changed it for the world.

For those hardy souls who participated in the aforementioned scenario I hope this book has revived some pleasant memories – for those who didn't, look what you missed out on!

An Afterthought

AH, THOSE OVERNIGHT travels. Nowadays when sleep evades me during the night hours my mind returns to those far off days/nights spent in the pursuit of steam. Perhaps its 11 p.m. or thereabouts and I can picture myself, a solitary enthusiast, waiting on the platform of a cold, windswept Lime Street station for the steam heated stock of the 23 38 Sunday night departure to arrive. Perhaps its nearer 2 a.m., with the ethereal refection of Sheffield Midland's station lights reflecting on a Jubilee with the Leeds departure. Or maybe it's nearer 3 a.m. – the memories of standing on an overcrowded one-coach departure out of Normanton bring a smile to my face. Finally, with dawn breaking, it's just gone 5 a.m., with the Hebden Bridge changeover about to ensue. None of these trains run today. The newspaper and mail traffic, together with the steam locomotives, are all gone – consigned to history books such as this. I console myself with the thought that I was young and able to undertake several consecutive nights 'on the chase' back then. I turn over, snuggle down under my warm duvet – the concurrent theme running through my head of 'I was there' – and sleep returns.

I find the present-day unit orientated national railway scene of insufficient interest to entice travels such as those detailed here. There have been many intervening years where family activities took priority and steam-locomotive chasing took a back seat. Over more recent times, however, with my daughter preferring foreign climes to here in the UK, the opportunities for a renewal of enthusiasm have been more available. The varieties of surviving locomotives operating on both main and preserved lines from a wide cross section of classes are a credit to all concerned. Throughout the country there are approximately 350 steam locomotives in the hands of the preservation movement – some are in pieces, some are a long way down the list of priorities for restoration, while others are very much alive and well. By my calculations the latter (subject to boiler tickets and failures) amount to about 270. Of these I still require runs with seventy-six (at the time of writing – 2015) so, therefore, taking into consideration some up-and-coming new builds, my hobby is still very much alive.

Holidays or weekend breaks can now be planned incorporating these 'needs' and, unlike the tales depicted throughout this book, can be caught while cherishing comfortable overnight accommodation between clean sheets – perhaps befitting my advancing years. My current stats are 1,243 locomotives for 99,795 miles – how are yours? I hope you have enjoyed the journeys I took you on back in the '60s and wish all those with similar interests a long and gratifying participation in a hobby that, courtesy of the stalwarts within the preservation movement, can continue to be relished by all and sundry.

On most family holidays over the years Joan, my ever understanding wife, always willingly acquiesces to a visit to the nearest preserved line. Having seen several 0-8-0-LNER Q6s during my journeys in the 1960s I had never travelled with one until, on 22 July 2008, the now preserved 63395, withdrawn at Sunderland forty-one years previously, was powering trains that day on the North Yorkshire Moors Railway. Here, at Grosmont, she readies herself for the 17¾ miles of undulating gradients ahead on her journey to Pickering – not bad for a 90-year-old!

An Afterthought

Two further visits were made to the former NER following steam's demise – both over lines which were to close. They were the Clayton West and Alston branches – the latter seen here being visited in August 1975.

A 'social' expedition to the Inner Hebrides in August 1987 was deliberately planned to include a return trip on what has become one of Scotland's biggest tourist attractions, that of the steam-operated 'Jacobite' trains over the West Highland line. Here at Mallaig on 30 August 1987 the now preserved K1 2-6-0 2005, a locomotive that had taken me on a tour of the Yorkshire Dales twenty years previously, rests having brought the morning train in from Fort William.

This LMS Fairburn 2-6-4T is one of two examples having survived the cutter's torch. A long way from her Cumbrian home, 42085, with whom I collected two runs when allocated to Manningham, is seen at Sheffield Park on 20 February 2010 while visiting the Bluebell railway.

Another survivor into the world of preservation was Patricroft's Standard 5MT 73096 – she having taken me over the Pennines in April 1967 on the Manchester/Leeds footex. Visiting Clapham Junction on a route clearance trial trip this Derby-built 43-year-old sets off back to her then home on the Mid Hants Railway on 27 January 1998.

With the only A1 in normal service having been viewed in a semi-derelict state at York in May 1966 this shot of new build 60163 *Tornado* in December 2009 indicates, to me, what a handsome design these locomotives were. She is seen arriving into Bromley South with a Christmas lunch circular tour of Kent and on this particular day was the *only* right-time running train in South East England – severe icing of the third rail having decimated normal services.

BEWARE
RAIL ENTHUSIASTS DISEASE

HIGHLY INFECTIOUS TO MALES OF ALL AGES

THE SYMPTOMS: The sufferer becomes confused and bewildered when not near a railway. Will be observed wandering around with blank expression, muttering strangewords. Rapid rise in temperature at sight of a train. Behaviour then becomes erratic: much rushing about and waving of arms. Foaming at the mouth is not unusual. Is sometimes violent to non-believers. The Patient spends much time and money at book and magazine shops. Seems not to notice presence of "Normal" people.

THIS CONDITION IS NOT FATAL

THE TREATMENT: Patient must be kept well supplied with items of railway interest. Should be encouraged to go on steam tours and to open-days where he can meet other victims of the illness and exchange ideas with them. Friends and relations can aid recovery with free transport, free beer and meals. In case of emergency contact your nearest preservation society.

A recent Christmas present! Nothing more needs to be said.

Glossary

Feedback from my first book, purchased by non-railway enthusiasts, revealed that some of the terminology and many of the abbreviations left them more than mystified. This is for them.

Adex	Advertised excursion	
BR	British Rail (ways)	1948–1997
BSK	Brake Standard Corridor	
C&HPR	Cromford & High Peak Railway	1830–1862
DL	Diesel Locomotive	
DMU	Diesel (mechanical) Multiple Unit	
ECML	East Coast Main Line (Kings Cross to Edinburgh via York)	
ECS	Empty Coaching Stock	
EL	Electric Locomotive	
ER	Eastern Region of BR	1948–1992
EWD	Each Weekday (Mondays to Saturdays)	
F	Power ratio for freight traffic	
FO	Fridays Only	
Footex	Advertised excursions run in connection with a football event	
FSO	Fridays and Saturdays Only	
G&SW	Glasgow & South Western Railway	1850–1922
GER	Great Eastern Railway	1862–1922
GCR	Great Central Railway	1897–1922
GWR	Great Western Railway	1833–1922
K&WVR	Keighley & Worth Valley Railway	
L&BER	Leeds & Bradford Extension Railway	1845–1851
LE	Light Engine	

LCGB	The Locomotive Club of Great Britain	
LMR	London Midland Region of BR	1948–1992
LMS	London Midland & Scottish Railway	1923–1947
LNER	London & North Eastern Railway	1923–1947
LNWR	London & North Western Railway	1846–1922
LT&S	London, Tilbury & Southend Railway	1854–1922
L&Y	Lancashire & Yorkshire Railway	1847–1922
M&LR	Manchester & Leeds Railway	1836–1847
MNA	Master Neverers Association (★)	
MO	Mondays Only	
Mogul	Locomotive wheel arrangement (2-6-0)	
MPD	Motive Power Depot – Shed	
MR	Midland Railway	1844–1922
MT	Mixed Traffic (passenger and freight)	
MX	Mondays Excepted (Tuesdays to Saturdays)	
N&CR	Newcastle & Carlisle Railway	1825–1862
NCB	National Coal Board	1947–1987
NER	North Eastern Railway OR	1854–1922
NER	North Eastern Region	1948–1967
NYMR	North Yorkshire Moors Railway	
P	Power ratio for passenger traffic	
Pacific	Locomotive wheel arrangement (4-6-2)	
RCTS	The Railway Correspondence & Travel Society	
SAL&MR	Sheffield, Ashton-under-Lyne & Manchester Railway	1841–1847
ScR	Scottish Region of BR	1948–1992
SLS	The Stephenson Locomotive Society	
SR	Southern Railway OR	1923–1947
SR	Southern Region of BR	1948–1992
SD&LUR	South Durham & Lancaster Union Railway	1856–1863
ST	Saddle Tank	
STN	Special Traffic Notice	
SuO	Sundays only	
SX	Saturdays excepted (Mondays to Fridays)	
T	Tank	
TPO	Travelling Post Office	
WCML	West Coast Main Line (Euston to Glasgow via Crewe)	
WD	War Department	
WR	Western Region of BR	1948–1992

Glossary

(★) – The MNA was a 'shadowy' organisation founded on a common desire to travel by train whilst avoiding paying for the privilege. On the plus side, however, on a great many 'last' occasions they cleaned up the locomotive involved, usually overnight prior to its final working, for the benefit of all.

Steam locomotive wheel arrangements	
0-6-0	
0-8-0	
2-6-0	First figure indicates number of leading wheels
2-6-2	
2-6-4	Second figure indicates number of powered and coupled driving wheels
2-8-0	
2-10-0	Third figure indicates number of trailing wheels
4-6-0	
4-6-2	

Appendix I

Steam sheds within the North Eastern Region of BR		
Date	Shed closed to steam	Running total
04/66		21
05/66	Consett (52K)	20
06/66	Tweedmouth (52D), Leeds Neville Hill (55H)	18
11/66	Farnley Junction (55C)	17
01/67	Stourton (55B), Mirfield (56D), Huddersfield Hillhouses (55G)	14
04/67	Bradford Manningham (55F)	13
05/67	South Blyth (52F)	12
06/67	York (50A), Hull Dairycoates (50B), Goole (50D), Wakefield (56A)	8
09/67	West Hartlepool (51C), North Blyth (52F), Sunderland (52G), Tyne Dock (52H)	4
10/67	Leeds Holbeck (55A), Low Moor (56F/55J)	2
11/67	Royston (55D)	1
01/68	Normanton (55E)	0

Appendix II

Steam allocations within the North Eastern Region of BR											
Origin	Power	Wheels	Design	Apr '66	Oct '66	Apr '67	Aug '67	Sep '67	Oct '67	Nov '67	Dec '67
LMS/BR	4MT	2-6-4T	Fairburn	28	26	22	15	11	-	-	-
LMS	4MT	2-6-4T	Stanier	3	3	2	2	1	-	-	-
LMS	4MT	2-6-4T	Fowler	2	-	-	-	-	-	-	-
LMS/BR	4MT	2-6-0	Ivatt	41	40	19	10	3	-	-	-
LMS/BR	5MT	4-6-0	Stanier	30	27	23	19	14	-	-	-
LMS	5P6F	4-6-0	Jubilee	10	8	5	3	2	2	1	-
LMS	8F	2-8-0	Stanier	49	42	37	25	19	9	-	-
LNER/BR	8P6F	4-6-2	A1	1	-	-	-	-	-	-	-
LNER	7P6F	2-6-2	V2	2	1	-	-	-	-	-	-
LNER/BR	5MT	4-6-0	B1	34	30	12	3	3	-	-	-
LNER/BR	5P6F	2-6-0	K1	31	28	19	5	1	1	1	1
LNER	6F	0-8-0	Q6	38	24	15	3	-	-	-	-
LNER	5F	0-6-0	J27	40	27	18	5	-	-	-	-
BR	3MT	2-6-0	Riddles	5	5	2	-	-	-	-	-
WD/BR	8F	2-8-0	Riddles	137	121	86	25	4	-	-	-
BR	9F	2-10-0	Riddles	15	13	5	-	-	-	-	-
			Total	466	395	265	115	58	12	2	1

Appendix III

Index of all steam journeys made on North Eastern Region metals
(**bold** – required; *Italics* – not required)

Date – 1966	Loco	Shed	Train	Miles	Remarks
Thu 31 Mar	45254	12A	16 37 Carlisle/Brad For Sq	105	
	45254	*12A*	*21 30 Brad For Sq/Leeds City*	*13½*	*For St Pan*
Fri 1 Apr	45204	55A	02 00 Sheff Mid/Leeds City	39½	
	42093	*55F*	*07 30 Brad For Sq/Leeds City*	*13½*	*For St Pan*
	42085	55F	08 57 Shipley/Leeds City	10¾	08 50 Brad For Sq/ St Pan
	61199	50A	11 40 Harrogate/Leeds Ctl	18¼	For Kings X
	45227	10A	13 52 Leeds City/Bingley	14¼	For Morecambe
	45193	10J	15 18 Leeds City/Skipton	26¼	For Morecambe
	70040	12A	16 30 Skipton/Hellifield	10	15 40 Brad For Sq/ Carlisle
	44758	10J	17 36 Hellifield/Skipton	10	16 18 Morecambe/ Leeds Cty
	44824	55A	18 43 Skipton/Morecambe	44	17 47 from Leeds City
Fri 13 May	44854	55A	02 00 Sheff Mid/Leeds City	39½	
	42161	55A	07 02 Brad For Sq/Leeds City	13½	For Penzance (1)
	44852	55A	16 45 Leeds Ctl/Doncaster	29¾	
	44770	6J	19 49 Wfield Wgate/Brad Ex	17	Portion off 16 20 KX/Leeds C
	42152	*55F*	*20 52 Brad For Sq/Shipley*	*2¾*	*For Bristol*
	42138	55F	21 43 Shipley/Leeds City	10¾	21 30 Brad For Sq/ St Pan
Sat 14 May	45647	55C	04 35 York/Leeds City	25½	

Date	Loco	Shed	Route	Miles	Notes
	61386	56F	13 41 Wfield Wgate/Brad Ex	17	Portion off 10 20 KX/Leeds C
	42142	56F	15 05 Brad Ex/Wfield Wgate	17	Portion for Leeds C/KX
	44853	55A	17 11 Wfield Wgate/S Elshall	11	16 45 Leeds C/Doncaster
	61161	56A	18 25 Wfield Wgate/Brad Ex	17	Portion off 15 25 KX/Leeds C
Sat 18 Jun	62011	52D	07 50 Alnmouth/Alnwick	3	
	62011	52D	08 09 Alnwick/Alnmouth	3	
	42189	55F	12 06 Leeds City/Brad For Sq	13½	10 39 ex-Sheff Mid
	45208	56D	13 05 Brad Ex/Wfield Wgate	17	Portion for Leeds C/KX
	43070	56A	13 41 Wfield Wgate/Brad Ex	17	Portion off 10 20 KX/Leeds C
	61240	56A	15 05 Brad Ex/Wfield Wgate	17	Portion for Leeds C/KX
	61022	56A	16 55 Wfield Wgate/Brad Ex	17	Portion off 13 40 KX/Leeds C
	42196	56F	19 10 Brad Ex/Halifax	8	15 25 ex-KX
Sat 25 Jun	45694	56A	13 25 Bpool N/Halifax	59¼	For Brad Ex
	42108	56A	15 35 Halifax/Leeds C	16¼	Portion off 13 25 ex-Bpool N
	42055	56F	17 05 Brad Ex/Wfield Wgate	17	Portion for Leeds C/KX
	43137	56A	18 25 Wfield Wgate/Brad Ex	17	Portion off 15 25 KX/Leeds C
Sat 2 Jul	45562	55C	04 35 York/Leeds City	25½	
	44828	55A	05 46 Leeds City/Brad For Sq	13½	00 05 ex-St Pan
	45565	56F	08 20 Brad Ex/Bridlington	92	
	42184	56F	08 20 Brad Ex/Bowling Jn	1¼	Banked Bridlington train
	44694	56D	13 35 Scarboro/Wfield Kgate	69½	For Manch Vic (2)
	45647	55C	19 27 Huddersfield/Brad Ex	19	10 29 ex-Poole
	42196	56F	Greetland Jn/Brad Ex	10	Piloted 10 29 ex-Poole
	42055	56F	21 02 Halifax/Brad Ex	8	19 35 ex-Stockport
	45304	9K	22 00 Brad Ex/Huddersfield	19	
Sat 9 Jul	45593	55A	02 25 Leeds City/Glasgow C	229½	21 20 ex-St Pan

Appendix III

Sat 16 Jul	**45697**	55A	02 00 Sheff Mid/Norm	28½	For Leeds City
	61189	56F	03 10 Norm/Halifax	22	02 10 York/Manch Vic
	44890	9D	04 38 Halifax/Heb Bridge	8¾	02 10 York/Manch Vic
	45062	9J	05 28 Heb Bridge/Norm	27¼	04 20 Manch Vic/York
	61319	50A	07 06 Norm/Cford Ctl	3½	04 20 Manch Vic/York
	44910	8L	08 05 Cford Ctl/Brighouse	20	For Bpool N
	44891	9D	09 36 Brighouse/Huddersfield	8¾	09 06 Brad Ex/Poole
	45562	55C	10 02 Huddersfield/Rhyl	95	09 15 Leeds C/Llandudno
	45581	55C	18 10 Sheff Mid/Brad Ex	53	10 29 ex-Poole
	42664	56F	Greetland Jn/Brad Ex	10	Piloted 10 29 ex-Poole
	42184	56F	21 02 Halifax/Brad Ex	8	19 35 ex-Stockport
	61224	56A	22 00 Brad Ex/Huddersfield	19	
Sat 23 Jul	**45675**	55A	02 00 Sheff Mid/Norm	28½	For Leeds City
	42204	56A	04 25 Norm/W'field Kgate	3	For Rochdale
	43070	56A	05 15 W'field Kgate/Barnsley	10¾	
	43070	56A	06 10 Barnsley/Wfield Kgate	10¾	
	45385	8F	06 42 Wfield Kgate/Norm	3	04 20 Manch Vic/York
	61199	50A	07 06 Norm/Cford Ctl	3½	04 20 Manch Vic/York
	45739	56A	08 05 Cford Ctl/Mirfield	12½	For Bpool N
	45593	55A	10 15 Leeds City/Carlisle	113	06 40 Bham/Glasgow C
Sat 30 Jul	**45697**	55A	02 25 Leeds City/Carlisle	113	21 20 St Pan/Glasgow C
Sat 27 Aug	*45675*	55A	02 00 Sheff Mid/Norm	28½	For Leeds City
	61022	56A	03 10 Norm/Halifax	22	02 10 York/Manch Vic
	45101	9D	04 38 Halifax/Heb Bridge	8¾	02 10 York/Manch Vic
	44962	8F	05 28 Heb Bridge/Norm	27¼	04 20 Manch Vic/York
	61019	50A	07 06 Norm/Cford Ctl	3½	04 20 Manch Vic/York

	44694	56F	08 05 Cford Ctl/Heb Bridge	30¾	For Bpool N	
Wed 31 Aug	45675	55A	02 00 Sheff M/Norm	28½	For Leeds City	
	61388	56F	03 10 Norm/Halifax	22	02 10 York/Manch Vic	
	45336	9D	04 38 Halifax/Heb Bridge	8¾	02 10 York/Manch Vic	
	45385	8F	05 28 Heb Bridge/Norm	27¾	04 20 Manch Vic/ York	
	61019	50A	07 06 Norm/York	24½	04 20 ex-Manch Vic	
	42141	55G	10 00 Brad Ex/Leeds C	9½	For KX (3)	
	42073	56F	11 00 Brad Ex/Leeds C	9½	For KX	
	42073	56F	13 41 Wfield Wgate/Brad Ex	17	Portion off 10 20 KX/Leeds C	
	42189	55F	16 30 Brad For Sq/Shipley	2¾	For Bham	
	42622	55A	16 43 Shipley/Brad For Sq	2¾	11 50 ex-St Pan	
	42622	55A	18 25 Shipley/Leeds City	10¾	18 10 Brad For Sq/ Derby Mid	
	42699	55A	20 23 Leeds City/Brad For Sq	13½	15 50 ex-St Pan	
	42204	56A	22 00 Brad Ex/Huddersfield	22		
Sat 3 Sep	42116	56F	19 35 Stockport/Brad Ex	45		
Sat 8 Oct	42204	56A	03 10 Norm/Halifax	22	02 10 York/Manch Vic	
	44949	9D	04 38 Halifax/Sow Bridge	3¾	02 10 York/Manch Vic	
	44679	8F	05 40 Sow Bridge/Norm	22¼	04 20 Manch Vic/ York	
	42149	55E	07 06 Norm/York	24½	04 20 ex-Manch Vic	
	42152	55F	10 15 Leeds City/Brad For Sq	13½	06 40 ex-Bham	
	90076	56A	Wfield Kgate/Goole	32	railtour	
	42942	8H	Goole/Wfield Kgate	27	railtour	
	44927	9K	18 25 Wfield Wgate/Brad Ex	17	Portion off 15 25 KX/Leeds C	
	42184	56F	21 02 Halifax/Brad Ex	8	19 30 ex-Stockport	
	61030	56A	22 00 Brad Ex/Huddersfield	19		
Sat 22 Oct	42184	56F	19 30 Stockport/Brad Ex	45		
	45197	10D	22 00 Brad Ex/Huddersfield	19		
Sat 5 Nov	42116	56F	19 30 Stockport/Brad Ex	45		
	42574	56A	22 00 Brad Ex/Huddersfield	19		

(1) – *The Cornishman*
(2) – D1542 piloted to York
(3) – *The Yorkshire Pullman*

Appendix III

Date – 1967	Loco	Shed	Train	Miles	Remarks
Sat 8 Apr	44990	56A	03 10 Norm/Halifax	22	02 10 York/Manch Vic
	45271	9D	04 38 Halifax/Heb Bridge	8¾	02 10 York/Manch Vic
	45075	55A	05 28 Heb Bridge/Norm	27¾	04 25 Manch Vic/York
	42073	56F	08 48 Halifax/Huddersfield	11	Portion for Leeds C/KX
	73096	9H	11 31 Manch Ex/Leeds City	43	Footex
	42235	56F	14 09 New Pudsey/Brad Ex	6	10 20 KX/Brad Ex (portion)
	42287	56A	15 05 Brad Ex/Wfield Wgate	17	Portion for Leeds C/KX
	45226	10D	16 28 Wfield Wgate/Brad Ex	17	Portion off 13 25 KX/Leeds C
	42085	55F	17 27 Brad For Sq/Leeds City	13½	For Sheff Mid
	73096	9H	18 15 Leeds City/Manch Ex	43	Footex
Sat 15 Apr	42055	56F	13 42 Wfield Wgate/Brad Ex	17	Portion off 10 20 KX/Leeds C
Sun 16 Apr	61994	PRES	Stockport/Keighley/Leeds C	88¾	rail tour
	41241	PRES	Haworth	4	
	60103	PRES	Leeds Central/Kings Cross	185¾	rail tour
Sat 22 Apr	44836	9B	03 10 Norm/Halifax	22	02 10 York/Manch Vic
	44891	9D	04 38 Halifax/Heb Bridge	8¾	02 10 York/Manch Vic
	45211	55A	05 28 Heb Bridge/Norm	27¾	04 25 Manch Vic/York
	43043	55E	07 06 Norm/York	24½	04 25 ex-Manch Vic
	42116	56F	11 00 Brad Ex/Leeds Ctl	9½	For KX
	42116	56F	13 42 Wfield Wgate/Brad Ex	17	Portion off 10 20 KX/Leeds C
	42574	56A	15 05 Brad Ex/Wfield Wgate	17	Portion for Leeds C/KX
	44826	55A	16 28 Wfield Wgate/Brad Ex	17	Portion off 13 25 KX/Leeds C
	42233	56F	17 20 Brad Ex/Leeds Ctl	9½	For KX
Sat 29 Apr	44846	9D	03 32 Leeds Ctl/Halifax	16¼	
	44846	9D	04 38 Halifax/Heb Bridge	8¾	02 10 York/Manch Vic

	45219	55A	05 28 Heb Bridge/Norm	27¾	04 25 Manch Vic/York
	45075	55A	07 58 Cudworth/Leeds City	21	07 06 ex-Sheff Mid
	44824	55A	10 05 Brad For Sq/Leeds City	13½	For Paignton (1)
	44826	55A	12 24 Wfield Wgate/New Pud	14½	09 25 KX/Brad Ex (portion)
	42196	56F	14 09 New Pud/Brad Ex	3½	10 20 ex-KX (portion)
Sat 20 May	42616	56F	03 10 Norm/Halifax	22	02 10 York/Manch Vic
	45203	9D	04 38 Halifax/Heb Bridge	8¾	02 10 York/Manch Vic
	44828	55A	05 28 Heb Bridge/Norm	27¾	04 25 Manch Vic/York
	42093	55E	07 06 Norm/York	24½	04 25 ex-Manch Vic
	62005	52F	Stockton/Darlington	112¼	rail tour
Fri 2 Jun	44911	12A	17 34 Manch Ex/York	68½	
Sat 10 Jun	42055	56F	03 10 Norm/Halifax	22	02 10 York/Manch Vic
	44846	9D	04 38 Halifax/Heb Bridge	8¾	02 10 York/Manch Vic
	45080	55A	05 28 Heb Bridge/Norm	27¾	04 25 Manch Vic/York
	44857	55A	07 06 Norm/York	24½	04 25 ex-Manch Vic
	45428	55A	Wfield Kgate/York	27½	rail tour
	45562	55A	York/Ashington	102¼	rail tour
	39	NCB	Ashington Colliery	4	rail tour
	45562	55A	Ashington/York	103½	rail tour
	45428	55A	York/Wfield Kgate	27½	rail tour
	42252	56F	22 04 Wfield Kgate/Huddersfield	14½	18 53 KX/Brad Ex (portion)
Sat 17 Jun	42283	56F	03 10 Norm/Halifax	22	02 10 York/Manch Vic
	44861	9D	04 38 Halifax/Manch Vic	32½	0 210 ex-York
Sat 24 Jun	42251	56F	03 10 Norm/Halifax	22	02 10 York/Manch Vic
	45203	9D	04 38 Halifax/Manch Vic	32½	02 10 ex-York
Sat 15 Jul	42066	56F	03 10 Norm/Halifax	22	02 10 York/Manch Vic
	45203	9D	04 38 Halifax/Manch Vic	32½	02 10 ex-York
Sat 22 Jul	45428	55A	07 06 Sheff Mid/Leeds City	39½	

Appendix III

	45593	55A	10 17 Leeds City/Carlisle	113	06 40 Bham/Glasgow C
Fri 4 Aug	**44817**	12A	17 47 Manch Ex/Leeds City	50¾	For York
	45219	55A	20 22 Leeds City/Manch Ex	43	For Holyhead
Fri 18 Aug	42141	56F	22 33 Huddersfield/Brad Ex	19	18 53 KX/Brad Ex (portion)
	44694	56F	23 55 Brad Ex/Leeds City	9½	For KX
Sat 19 Aug	45203	9D	04 38 Halifax/Manch Vic	32½	02 10 ex-York
Sat 26 Aug	45198	8F	08 25 Manch Vic/Huddersfield	25¾	For Scarborough
	45562	55A	10 17 Leeds City/Carlisle	113	06 40 Bham/Glasgow C
Sun 27 Aug	73073	9H	23 38 Lpool Lime St/Leeds City	74	For York
Mon 28 Aug	**44775**	12A	03 32 Leeds City/Halifax	16¼	
	44775	12A	04 38 Halifax/Manch Vic	32½	02 10 ex-York
Tue 29 Aug	70004	12A	12 20 Carlisle/Leeds City	113	09 56 Glasgow C/St Pan
Fri 1 Sep	**44825**	12A	17 47 Manch Ex/Leeds City	50¾	For York
	45208	56F	20 45 Brad Ex/Leeds City	9½	For Paignton
	42152	55A	22 04 Wfield Kgate/Brad Ex	33½	18 53 KX/Brad Ex (portion)
	45208	56F	23 55 Brad Ex/Leeds City	9½	For KX
Sat 2 Sep	42141	56F	03 10 Norm/Halifax	22	02 10 York/Manch Vic
	44949	9D	04 38 Halifax/Manch Vic	32½	02 10 ex-York
Sat 30 Sep	42689	56F	03 10 Norm/Halifax	22	02 10 York/Manch Vic
	45287	8A	04 38 Halifax/Heb Bridge	8¾	02 10 York/Manch Vic
	44971	10D	07 58 Cudworth/Leeds City	21	07 06 ex-Sheff Mid
	61306	56F	09 55 Brad Ex/Leeds City	9½	For KX (2)
	45428	55A	14 20 Leeds City/Brad Ex	9½	
	45428	55A	16 50 Leeds City/New Pudsey	6	13 25 KX/Brad Ex (portion)
Sat 14 Oct	**45221**	8B	03 32 Leeds City/Halifax	16¼	
	45221	8B	04 38 Halifax/Manch Vic	32½	02 10 ex-York
Sun 22 Oct	73053	9H	23 38 Lpool Lime St/Leeds City	76	For York
Sat 28 Oct	70013	12A	Manch Vic/Norm	117	rail tour
	45562	55A	Norm/Norm	47¾	rail tour
	70013	12A	Norm/Rose Grove	54½	rail tour
Fri 3 Nov	45203	9D	04 38 Halifax/Manch Vic	32½	02 10 ex-York

	70051	12A	17 47 Manch Ex/York	76	
Sat 4 Nov	45203	9D	03 32 Leeds City/Halifax	16¼	
	45203	9D	04 38 Halifax/Heb Bridge	8¾	02 10 York/Manch Vic
	60019	PRES	08 45 Leeds City/Edinburgh	230¼	rail tour
Sun 5 Nov	73128	9H	23 38 Lpool Lime St/Patricroft	26¼	For York
Mon 6 Nov	73132	9H	01 00 Patricroft/Leeds City	47¾	23 38 Lpool/York

(1) – *The Devonian*
(2) – *The Yorkshire Pullman*

Date – 1968	Loco	Shed	Train	Miles	Remarks
Sat 20 Jan	44949	9D	03 32 Leeds City/Halifax	16¼	
	44949	9D	04 38 Halifax/Manch Vic	32½	02 10 ex-York
Sat 10 Feb	45310	9D	03 32 Leeds City/Halifax	16¼	
	45310	9D	04 38 Halifax/Manch Vic	32½	02 10 ex-York
Sat 30 Mar	44910	9D	03 32 Leeds City/Halifax	16¼	
	44910	9D	04 38 Halifax/Manch Vic	32½	02 10 ex-York
Sat 27 Apr	45310	9D	03 32 Leeds City/Halifax	16¼	
	45310	9D	04 38 Halifax/Manch Vic	32½	02 10 ex-York
	73050 **73069**	9H	Stalybridge/Bolton	72¼	rail tour

NON-RESIDENTIAL STEAM LOCOMOTIVES CAUGHT ON NER METALS = 46
HOME-ALLOCATED NER STEAM LOCOMOTIVES CAUGHT = 73

Total 119

Index to shed codes: 5B – Crewe South, 6J – Holyhead, 8A – Edge Hill, 8B – Warrington Dallam, 8F – Springs Branch, 8H – Birkenhead, 8L – Aintree, 9B – Stockport Edgeley, 9D – Newton Heath, 9J – Agecroft, 9K – Bolton, 9H – Patricroft, 10A – Carnforth, 10D – Lostock Hall, 10J – Lancaster Green Ayre, 12A – Carlisle Kingmoor, 50A – York, 52D – Tweedmouth, 52F – North/South Blyth, 55A – Leeds Holbeck, 55C – Farnley Junction, 55E – Normanton, 55F – Bradford Manningham, 55G – Huddersfield Hillhouses, 56A – Wakefield, 56D – Mirfield, 56F (55J) – Bradford Low Moor, PRES – Preserved (privately owned).

Appendix IV

1966 – The Indian summer for the 'Jubilees'				
No.	Name	Allocation	Caught	Withdrawn
45562	Alberta	55C/55A	Jul '66, Jun/Aug/Oct 67	04/11/67
45565	Victoria	56F	Jul '66	06/01/67
45581	Bihar and Orissa	55C	Jul '66	07/08/66
45593	Kolhapur	55A	Aug '65, Jun/Jul '66, Jul '67	15/10/67
45647	Sturdee	55C/55A	May/Jul '66	26/04/67
45675	Hardy	55A	Jul/Aug '66	24/06/67
45694	Bellerophon	56A	Jun '66	04/01/67
45697	Achilles	55A	Jul '66	05/08/67
45739	Ulster	56A	Jul '66	04/01/67

Alberta is a west Canadian prairie province; Victoria, at sixty-three years seven months, was the longest serving British monarch (so far); Bihar and Orissa were provinces of British India (1912–36); Kolhapur is a city on India's Arabian Sea coast; Sturdee was a British admiral (1859–1925) who fought in the First World War at the battles of the Falkland Islands and Jutland; Hardy was a Royal Naval Officer (1790-1839); Bellerophen, Achilles were Royal Navy Ships; Ulster is a province of Northern Ireland.

Services rostered for Jubilee haulage during the summer of 1966		
Depot	Train	Remarks
55A	02 00 Sheffield Midland/Leeds City	
55A	02 25 Leeds City/Carlisle	21 20 St Pancras/Glasgow
55C	04 35 York/Leeds City	
56A	08 05 Castleford Ctl/Blackpool North	& 13 25 return to Bradford Ex
56F	08 20 Bradford Ex/Bridlington	& 13 25 return
55C	09 08 Leeds City/Nottingham Midland	For Poole – & return (to Bradford Ex)
55A	09 15 Leeds City/Llandudno	& 15 25 return
55A	10 17 Leeds City/Carlisle	06 40 Birmingham/Glasgow

Appendix V

Two Sample Summer Forays (NER Extracts Only)

Saturday 2 July 1966				
Time (arr. dep.)	Location	Traction	Notes	Miles
04 35	York	45562 (55C)	*Alberta*	
05 09 05 58	Leeds City	44828 (55A)		25½
	00 05 ex-St Pancras			
06 19	Bradford Forster Square			13½
08 20	Bradford Exchange	45565 (56F)	*Victoria*	
	Banked to Bowling Jn by 42184 (56F)			
11 46 12 00	Bridlington	DMU		92
12 40 13 35	Scarborough Central	44694 (56D)		22¾
	Piloted to York by D1542			
	For Manchester Exchange			
15 27 15 35	Wakefield Kirkgate	DMU		69½
16 39 17 09	Sheffield Midland	44846 (9D)		27
	11 55 ex-Yarmouth Vauxhall			
18 18	Manchester Victoria			46¾
18 45	Manchester Exchange	DMU		
19 29 19 39	Huddersfield	45647 (55C)	*Sturdee*	26
	10 29 ex-Poole			
	Piloted from Greetland Jn by 42196 (56F)			

Time (arr. dep.)		Location	Traction	Notes	Miles
20 18	20 38	Bradford Exchange	DMU		19
20 44	21 02	Halifax	42055 (56F)		8
		19 35 ex-Stockport Edgeley			
21 18	22 00	Bradford Exchange	45304 (9K)		8
22 53		Huddersfield			19

Saturday 16 July 1966					
Time (arr. dep.)		Location	Traction	Notes	Miles
	02 00	Sheffield Midland	45697 (55A)	*Achilles*	
		For Leeds City			
03 00	03 10	Normanton	61189 (56F)	*Sir William Gray*	28½
		02 10 York/Manchester Victoria			
		Halifax	44890 (9D)		22
05 00	05 30	Hebden Bridge	45062 (9J)		8¾
		04 20 Manchester Victoria/York			
		Normanton	61319 (50A)		27¼
07 15	08 05	Castleford Central	44910 (8L)		3½
		For Blackpool North			
09 04	09 36	Brighouse	44891 (9D)		20
		09 06 Bradford Exchange/Poole			
09 55	10 22	Huddersfield	45562 (55C)	*Alberta*	7
		09 15 Leeds City/Llandudno			
13 15	13 58	Rhyl	73006 (9H)		95
		13 15 ex-Llandudno			
16 15		Manchester Exchange			70
	17 00	Manchester Piccadilly	27004	*Juno*	
17 59		Sheffield Victoria			41½
	18 11	Sheffield Midland	45581 (55C)	*Bihar & Orissa*	
		10 29 ex-Poole			
		Piloted from Greetland Jn by 42664 (56F)			
20 15	20 30	Bradford Exchange	DMU		58
20 43	21 02	Halifax	42184 (56F)		8
		19 35 ex-Stockport Edgeley			
21 20	22 00	Bradford Exchange	61224 (56A)		8
22 53		Huddersfield			19

Appendix VI

Railways Across the Pennines

Year opened	Route	Company (★)	Current status
1830	Cromford & High Peak	C&HPR	Closed 1967
1838	Newcastle & Carlisle	N&CR	Open
1841	Calder Valley	M&LR	Open
1845	Woodhead	SAL&MR	Closed 1981
1848	Standedge	LNWR	Open
1848	Colne & Skipton	L&BER	Closed 1970
1849	Copy Pit	L&YR	Open
1861	Stainmore	SD&LUR	Closed 1962
1863	Whaley Bridge/Buxton	LNWR	Open
1867	Chinley/Matlock	MR	Closed 1968
1876	Settle/Carlisle	MR	Open
1894	Hope Valley	MR	Open

(★) for company descriptions see glossary

Appendix VII

Preserved Railways in the North East of England

Please visit these railways and support the efforts of the volunteers who willingly give their time to recreate the steam railway lost in the 1960s. Without them the heritage industry would be that much poorer and future generations would never be able to participate and enjoy the pleasures of steam-train travel:

Aln Valley Railway, Bowes Railway, Derwent Valley Light Railway, Eden Valley Railway, Elsecar Heritage Railway, Embsay and Bolton Abbey Steam Railway, Kirklees Light Railway, Middleton Railway, North Tyndale Steam Railway, North Yorkshire Moors Railway, Keighley and Worth Valley Railway, South Tyneside Railway, Stainmore Railway, Tanfield Railway, Weardale Railway, Wensleydale Railway, Yorkshire Wolds Railway.

Sources

Glossop Guild (Appendix VI)
Ian Allan *British Railways Gradient Profiles*
The Railway World magazine
Ian Allan *1966 Trains Annual*
The *LCGB Monthly Bulletin*
The Engine Shed Society – *BR Steam Locomotive Sheds and Allocations*
Longworth, Hugh, *BR Steam Locomotives 1948–1968*
BR Database

Unless otherwise stated all images are from my collection. To view my website please visit http://mistermixedtraction.smugmug.com, then select one of twenty galleries – 'The Orange Zone' being particularly relevant to this book. Simply click on 'slideshow', sit back and enjoy. Anyone wishing to purchase copies of the images contained here please visit www.railwayimages.com where, under featured photographers, you will find my name and all my photographs of the final five years of BR steam.

If you enjoyed this book, you may also be interested in …

The Great Steam Chase

KEITH WIDDOWSON

978 0 7524 7957 6

Amassing over 52,000 miles from Kent to Cornwall, here is the story of Keith Widdowson's journey as he raced against time to chronicle the steam locomotives working throughout southern England before they succumbed to modern traction. From sleep deprivation to gung-ho drivers, this is no ordinary trainspotter's diary but a nostalgic and evocative look back at how things really were in those steam days. A must-have for enthusiasts and locals to the closed railways alike, this is one man's journey, with 140 contemporary images to capture the railway as it was then, fully aware that things were about to change for good (but not necessarily for the better). From closing branch lines to final steam workings, here is the last snapshot of the golden age of steam. It is a personal and informed account that all people with any interest in the Southern Region or steam in general will no doubt relate to.

Visit our website and discover thousands of other History Press books.

www.thehistorypress.co.uk